CRAFTED IN BRITAIN

The Survival of Britain's Traditional Industries

Bloomsbury Publishing

An imprint of Bloomsbury Publishing Plc

50 Bedford Square	1385 Broadway
London	New York
WC1B 3DP	NY 10018
UK	USA

www.bloomsbury.com

BLOOMSBURY and the Diana logo are trademarks of Bloomsbury Publishing Plc

First published 2017

© Anthony Burton and Rob Scott, 2017

British Library Cataloguing-in-Publication Data
A catalogue record for this book is available from the British Library.

Library of Congress Cataloguing-in-Publication data has been applied for.

ISBN: HB: 978-1-4729-2283-0
ePDF: 978-1-4729-2282-3
ePub: 978-1-4729-2281-6

2 4 6 8 10 9 7 5 3 1

Designed and typeset in Haarlemmer by Simon Bishop Design
Printed in China by RRD Asia Printing Solutions Limited

Bloomsbury Publishing Plc makes every effort to ensure that the papers used in
the manufacture of our books are natural, recyclable products made from wood grown in
well-managed forests. Our manufacturing processes conform to the environmental
regulations of the country of origin.

To find out more about our authors and books visit www.bloomsbury.com.
Here you will find extracts, author interviews, details of forthcoming events
and the option to sign up for our newsletters.

CRAFTED IN BRITAIN

The Survival of Britain's Traditional Industries

WORDS BY ANTHONY BURTON
PHOTOGRAPHS BY ROB SCOTT

BLOOMSBURY
LONDON · OXFORD · NEW YORK · NEW DELHI · SYDNEY

Contents

Introduction

In the 19th century Britain was often described as the workshop of the world. But even as early as 1837 a former Prime Minister, Benjamin Disraeli, was prophesying that the rest of the world would not accept that situation for ever, though it is doubtful if anyone in Victorian Britain could have foreseen that in the 20th century another Prime Minister, Margaret Thatcher, would publicly turn her back on the whole concept in favour of 'service industries'. When industries decline, it is not just material things that are lost, but a whole world of expertise and craftsmanship. Yet in spite of the drastic decline in Britain's traditional crafts and industries, some survive, preserving skills and technologies developed in some cases over many centuries. It is these survivors that this book celebrates.

It could be argued that the world has moved on in recent decades and to look back on former triumphs is no more than an enjoyable but ultimately futile exercise in nostalgia. The crafts, trades and industries that we shall be looking at, however, are not museum pieces: they have survived because they offer something valuable, something for which there is a continuing demand. In many cases this may be because people still appreciate the extra craftsmanship that produces artefacts which stand out from the general run of mass-produced objects. In a few cases, conservation work absolutely requires that older technologies be used so that the end product will fit comfortably next to the original work. In other instances, technology simply cannot replace human skills.

There is a good case to be made for celebrating these survivors, but why bother to describe the processes by which they are made? Much of our modern world is incomprehensible in its detail. A modern mobile phone is a wondrous thing – but you can't take it to pieces and see exactly how it works. One of the great fascinations of older technologies is that they are basically comprehensible. If you visit a watermill, for example, the machinery may look complex, but it doesn't take long to work out what does what. Water makes the wheel turn – that cog meshes with that cog, which in turn meshes with another, until eventually the grindstone itself is moved, and grain can be poured in and turned into flour. The processes are often as attractive and appealing as the end result. That is what we hope this book shows – not only a range of things that are in themselves intrinsically interesting but also the great fascination to be had from seeing just how they are made and how they function.

For both me and the photographer Rob there were surprises and delights along the way: it was extraordinary, for example, to see craftsmen turn a strip of silver into a beautifully shaped spoon and neither of us will ever forget the extraordinary atmosphere of the bell foundry and the feeling that it must have been much the same a century ago. Our hope is that in words and pictures we can share these and other wonderful experiences with the reader.

Food for the Table

The Grain Mill and the Millwright

Food is the most basic of all human requirements; without it we die. And no form of food is more basic than bread; there is evidence that cereals were being grown for food back in the Stone Age. Originally, the grain would have been crushed by hand by rubbing between two stones, but this was also one of the first processes ever to be mechanised. For many, many centuries the only way to produce flour was to use stones in some sort of mill. Inevitably, changes came and new types of mill appeared, producing white flour that was considered more refined, in every sense of the word, and more sophisticated. But the old mills producing wholegrain flour have survived – and the end product is now generally seen as offering a healthier option, not to mention a far better flavour. But there are very few mills that are still powered by water or wind that are actually working as fully commercial concerns, rather than relying on paying visitors to keep them going. Claybrooke Mill is one of them.

Claybrooke Mill in Leicestershire can be found very close to High Cross, a spot at the very heart of Roman Britain, the point where the two great roads, the Fosse Way and Watling Street, intersect. This is rather appropriate, as it was the Romans who first introduced the water mill to Britain. The earliest mills were very simple: paddle wheels on a vertical shaft were set directly in a stream, and turned the stones above them by direct drive. The Romans improved on this system, with a vertical wheel on a horizontal shaft – the type of wheel we all recognise today. It was first described in the 1st century BC by Vitruvius, and it sometimes known, perhaps rather pedantically, as the Vitruvian wheel. It was an immediate success, and by the time the Normans had conquered England and recorded their assets in the Domesday Book, they were able to list literally thousands of water mills producing grain. Claybrooke was one of those mills. It will have been rebuilt, modified and enlarged many times over the years, but it remains a remarkable story of continuity – millers have been working here doing much the same job for more than a thousand years.

The present mill may not have been here in medieval times, but it still has a long history that you can see in the building itself. At one end, the walls are built of typical multi-shaded 18th-century bricks, and this part probably dates from the 1780s. The other end has more uniform, machine-made 19th-century

Spencer Craven inspecting the grain as it pours down to the pair of millstones at Claybrooke Mill.

10

Claybrooke Mill stands on a site where milling has continued for a thousand years. The internal waterwheel is to the right of the building.

Above: A worn stencil used for marking sacks suggests that the mill might once have had a connection with the infamous Guy Fawkes.

Opposite: Checking the quality of the flour produced by the millstones on the floor above.

bricks from an extension in the 1840s. But the story really starts over a mile away, where the leat, the channel that supplies the mill, leaves a tributary of the river Soar. It arrives at a small pond at the back of the mill, and from here sluice gates can be opened to allow the water to turn the wheel. An important part of the miller's job is controlling the water supply: it is not something that can just be left alone. Without proper controls you run the risk of either letting the leat dry up by running too much off, or flooding.

This mill has an overshot wheel, one in which, instead of water pushing paddles at the rim, it drops into buckets set round the edge. It is the weight of water on one side that provides the power, and experiments in the 18th century showed this to be the most efficient type of water wheel. The wheel itself is enclosed at the end of the mill, and it's here that things start to get really interesting. The problem (that millwrights solved centuries ago) was how to convert the movement of the water wheel round its horizontal axle into the movement of the stones round their vertical axle. At the same time, it was very helpful if something could be done to make the stones move faster than the slowly turning wheel. The answer was to introduce complex gears, and you could argue that the water mill was probably the most complex piece of machinery that existed until the Industrial Revolution.

The first gear is the pit wheel, a large, toothed wheel that turns with the water wheel at the same speed. This engages with a bevelled wheel, the wallower, mounted on a vertical shaft. So that's the first part of the job done. Higher up the vertical shaft is a much bigger spur wheel. At each side of this are two small cogs, the stone nuts. It is the gear ratios that make the difference in speed: the steady rate of the water wheel is 9 rpm but the stone nuts turn their shafts at a nippy 100 rpm.

The action now moves up to the next floor and the grindstones themselves. There are two pairs, but only one is in use at any one time. These are not simply round stones. The lower bed stone is fixed, and only the runner above it turns. Each stone is cut with a complex of grooves. As the grain drops through the eye in the centre, it is sliced ever more finely as it gradually moves out to the edge of the circle to emerge as flour. These stones are French burrs, generally regarded as the finest millstones available. They are incredibly hard. The grooves have to be dressed – given clean edges – at roughly 12-monthly intervals. Modern tools are simply not up to the job: even a powered diamond cutter packs up before long. So the miller has to do as his forebears have done – work by hand with a mill bill, rather like a chisel mounted on a wooden handle like a hammer. Even this is not straightforward. The miller uses a staff, a wooden baton that is kept in the mill at all times to ensure it is kept at the same temperature and humidity as the stones. The top stone has to be lifted, using a simple rope and chain – not the easiest job, as it weighs around a ton. Then the staff is run over the surface to reveal any high spots that need to be smoothed away. The stones are also slightly dished so that the grain moves outwards, and this is a critical factor that depends entirely on the keen eye of the miller.

Spencer Craven took over the mill some 15 years ago, and the previous owner gave him a rudimentary lesson: how to start the whole thing working and how to stop it. The rest he had to find out for himself by trial and error. He soon discovered that making flour was not simply a matter of starting the wheels turning and pouring in grain. The grain itself is kept in bins on the top

floor and comes down a chute to a point above the stones. It is then directed into the eye of the stones by a second, smaller chute. This is agitated to shake in the grain by means of the damsel. This is a bulbous metal rod that spins round, clattering against the side of the chute. The very non-PC explanation of the name is that it is forever chattering like a young lady. The angle of the chute can be adjusted to increase the speed at which the grain flows down.

The miller has to perform a balancing act: the faster the grain hits the stones, the more power is needed to complete the job. The only way to tell when things are going just as they should is to pop down to the ground floor and test the flour. The testing device has never changed: it is known as the miller's golden thumb. Only by rubbing the flour between forefinger and thumb can he assess how well things are going. This is not a job for the idle,

constantly going up and down the steep stairs to make the small adjustments that make for the perfect flour.

No amount of adjustment, however, will produce the perfect wholemeal flour unless the grain is right for the job. The wheat can be ordered using two different systems. There is a highly regulated system, where you specify your needs and order a specific reference number. There is, however, no means of knowing where the wheat has originated: it is as likely to come from Russia or Canada as from a field in Britain. And many of these wheats are hard. Spencer Craven discovered quite early on that if he wanted the right wheat for his mill, he should be looking for names, not numbers. Then he got a much softer wheat, perfect for stone milling: during our visit he was using a grain called "Paragon" that came from neighbouring Warwickshire. This

Above: The finished product: flour bagged and ready for sale.

Opposite: The power house of the mill: the large vertical pit wheel engages with the horizontal wallower to turn the shaft that leads to the floor above and the millstones. The mechanism is being greased to ensure smooth running.

was the wheat that had finished its journey through the mill and was pouring down from the stones into a sack on the ground floor. This really is wholemeal: everything goes in, so that you get not just the soft kernel but also the fibrous bran as well as the essential oils. It is always difficult to escape the general feeling that 'natural' is necessarily synonymous with 'healthy', but there seems to be a growing body of genuine scientific evidence that flour such as this really does have genuine health benefits. And if you have ever wondered what the difference is between wholemeal and white flour, the mill has the answer to that as well. The flour can be run through a bolter, a cylinder of cloth that can be rotated, acting rather like a centrifuge. The finer matter goes through the cloth; the rest is left behind. For every 25kg of wholemeal that goes in, just 10kg of white flour comes out; or, to put it another way, most of the grain is discarded. Not everyone is concerned about health issues. There is, however, another argument in favour of wholemeal, stone-ground flour: the bread you make from it tastes far better.

Left: Willesbrough windmill, a wooden smock mill with a rotating cap.

Opposite: Vincent Pargeter at work at the top of the mill, standing next to the shaft that is attached directly to the sails.

the whole structure had to be swung round. Later, a more sophisticated version was developed, in which the sails were mounted on a rotating cap at the top of the mill. It was no longer even necessary to haul the whole thing round manually. A fantail, a device rather like a child's oversized whirligig, was mounted on the opposite side of the cap to the sails. When the sails were correctly positioned, the blades were shielded from the wind, but if the wind direction shifted, the blades began to turn, driving the cap round automatically. When you 'get it', there is something deeply satisfying about the fantail: an entirely self-adjusting feedback system. It was patented in 1745 by Edmund Lee, a Lancashire blacksmith. Imagine him inviting a group of millers to witness the first demonstration.

There is one more factor that has to be brought into play. Just as the sails of a sailing ship have to be adjusted to allow for different strengths of wind, so too do the sails of a windmill. The earliest versions had cloth-covered sails that could be reefed in, but later mills had sails made of adjustable shutters, rather like a Venetian blind.

Both types of mill were complex to build and maintain. This was the work of the millwright, arguably the original mechanical engineer; it still is. Vincent Pargeter started off in a very different occupation, working in the planning department of Essex County Council. Working on windmills was a hobby, which began with the restoration of the White windmill at Sandwich on the Isle of Wight. In 1969, after eight years of working as a volunteer, he felt he had acquired sufficient expertise to set up as a full-time millwright. He was to stay in the job for the rest of his life.

We met up with Vincent when he was working at restoring Willesborough windmill at Ashford in Kent. This is one of the mills with a rotating cap, known as a smock mill, because the main body of the mill is made of wood; mills built of stone or brick are tower mills. Vincent had to master a wide range of skills. He was an expert carpenter and had his own forge for making iron parts. He was prepared to do anything that needed doing, from painting the outside to resetting the gears. He even had to design a whole new set of machinery for a derelict mill, originally built by Holman Brothers of Canterbury. It was a long way from their home base – it stands in the old city of Jerusalem.

Just as this book was nearing completion, we heard the sad news that Vincent had passed away. It seemed appropriate, however, to still give him his place in this book, though he has a more lasting memorial: the many, many mills that turn again thanks to his efforts.   CB

The alternative to the water mill was the windmill, developed in Britain rather later than the water mill: the earliest reference is to a mill at Weedley in Yorkshire in 1185. The machinery of the mill is similar in many ways to that of the water mill, except that it is the other way up, with the power source at the top instead of at the bottom. The windmill, however, has a problem that is not shared with the water mill: in order for it to work, the sails have to be faced into the changing wind. The earliest solution was the post mill. In this, the buck, the structure containing the whole of the machinery, was mounted on a central post. In order to bring it into the wind,

The
Cheese Maker

What better traditional accompaniment to a fine wholemeal loaf could you have than a tasty British cheese? Cheese might well be the earliest processed food. No one can be quite sure, simply because no one really knows just when it was first made, but it has certainly been around for a few thousand years. One of the earliest written mentions comes in a biblical story: David was out delivering cheeses to the army when he first encountered Goliath. But it was to be a long time before cheese arrived in Britain, where it first appeared as part of the basic rations of the Roman legions. The British took to this new foodstuff with enthusiasm, and over the centuries different regions developed their own methods of making cheese. There were two main varieties: cheese made from cow's milk, which was enjoyed by the aristocracy, and ewe's milk cheese, which was what the rest of the population ate. There were also small quantities of goat's milk cheese made. Bread and cheese became major ingredients in the diet of a large part of the population – and they were very nutritious too. Cheese is rich in protein and essential minerals, particularly calcium. Today, if you visit any supermarket you will find British cheeses sitting alongside others from Europe, especially France, Italy and Holland. For a time it was thought to be quite the thing to put a foreign cheese on your table, far more exotic than the humble home-grown, and therefore almost by definition inferior, varieties. Yet in the Middle Ages, continental Europe was buying large quantities of cheese from Britain, and there are records of Cotswold cheeses being exported from Southampton. The story of Gloucestershire cheeses is typical of the history of many other varieties.

Robert Smith in his excellent book *The Great Cheeses of Britain and Ireland* gives a useful potted history of the county's cheese making. The first Gloucestershire cheeses were made from ewe's milk and apparently there were 1,700 sheep grazing on Minchinhampton Common, Stroud, at the beginning of the 14th century: in just one summer over 3000 lb of cheese was recorded as being made from the milk of these flocks. By 1498, cheese making was considered so important that Gloucester opened a specialist cheese market, and the export market for the produce was soon rivalling the other major industry of the region, woollen cloth. One reason for the success was the local breed of Gloucester cattle, whose milk had a

Mrs Diana Smart cutting up the junket, the clotted milk, as it starts to form. There is a row of cheese presses behind her.

Above: The full cream milk ready for cheese making.

Opposite: Rod Smart breaking up the curd using a wooden hay rake.

very high fat content, perfect for making strongly flavoured, rich cheese. A disastrous cattle plague in the 18th century almost wiped out the old breed, and it was mainly replaced by different stock, whose milk was fine for drinking but less satisfactory for cheese. But the real decline began in the following century. Cheap imports and the high prices being paid by customers for milk persuaded many farmers to abandon cheese making altogether. By the middle of the 20th century, virtually all Gloucestershire cheese making had come to an end. But recent years have seen a revival, and one of the pioneers was Mrs Diana Smart, who began making true Double Gloucester and Single Gloucester, and still does, now working in partnership with her son Rod.

The Smart farm can be found just to the west of Gloucester at Birdwood. The village lies on the busy A40, but to reach the farm you have to turn down a very narrow single-track road and then bump your way up the long drive to reach the farm itself. This is a working farm, not a show farm, a higgledy-piggledy array of barns and outbuildings, made out of whatever material happened to be handy at the time, from timber and brick to breeze block and corrugated iron. Hens scratch among the straw, dogs bark a welcome rather than a warning, and the lowing of cows is mingled with the more distant grunt of pigs. It is one of those farms that appear ramshackle, but where the owners know exactly where everything is and what to do with it. The actual cheese making takes place in one of the outbuildings, and here the apparent chaos gives way to order. All visitors have to dunk their shoes in disinfectant baths before entering, an imperative for modern hygiene, but everywhere else tradition is the order of the day.

The first stage is to heat the milk and stir it constantly to prevent the cream settling out – once it has floated to the top you can't put it back in; no amount of later mixing will make a homogeneous cream milk. A starter is added. This is a bacterium or mixture of bacteria, which starts the work of turning the natural lactose in the milk into lactic acid. The next ingredient to be added is rennet. This is one of those mysterious substances that leave one wondering how on earth anyone ever discovered it could be used in cheese making in the first place. It is a clotting agent, and traditionally it comes from the fourth stomach of a calf. There is something reassuringly precise about the nomination of the stomach – obviously all other stomachs are quite inferior. Eventually it was discovered that other sources could be used, and the rennet can be made from vegetable, not animal, sources. Once the rennet has been added, the milk starts to clot to form a junket. After about three-quarters of an hour the junket is cut by knives, which aren't really knives at all, but fine-meshed screens. One other even more exotic ingredient is added, annatto, made from the seed coat of a South American tree. It is a natural colouring agent that gives Double Gloucester its attractive reddish-orange tinge.

Now the mixture in the hot vat has to be kept constantly on the move, as the curd begins to break down into ever-smaller pieces. It is a very hypnotic process. Rod Smart uses a wooden hay rake, which is constantly passed to and fro through the vat, sending creamy yellow waves rolling backwards and forwards. This goes on for at least 45 minutes for the Double, but half an

hour does for the thinner Single mixture. Deciding just when to stop this process is a question of judgement, and it is something a good cheese maker will learn until it is almost second nature. All he or she has to do is crumble the curd between the fingers and assess the texture. When the moment is right, the whey is run off. It is not wasted. It is pumped into a tank and a lot of it finds an excellent use. It goes to the Gloucester Old Spot pigs, which are as traditional a part of the local scene as the cheese. They love it. As soon as it's poured into the trough, they are in there, shoving and pushing, and if necessary giving a little nip on the ear of a neighbour, as each pig fights for its share of the tasty liquid. This is good, natural food for the pigs, which in summer

root around in the orchard. It all gives flavour to the end product, and helps explain just why Old Spot bacon is about as good as it gets.

For a Double Gloucester, full cream milk is used. Single Gloucester is rather different, and has its origins in the comparatively distant past. Cows naturally produce more milk in spring than in the rest of the year, and it became something of a glut on the market. So the milk was left out for the cream to separate. It was skimmed off and the skimmed milk added to full cream milk to make a lighter cheese. It was generally not considered suitable for sale to the better-class customers, but was just the thing for workers at harvest time. Both varieties are made, each batch of 150 gallons of

Above: Cheeses slowly maturing in the storeroom.

Left: Cutting the curd into slabs.

Opposite: Gloucester Old Spot pigs eagerly awaiting their treat of whey.

milk producing 180 lb of cheese. The process is long and quite complex and the result depends to a very large extent on the skill and experience of the cheese maker.

Once all the whey is gone, the curd is cut – this time using a conventional knife – into blocks of ever-decreasing size that are piled on top of each other and gently pressed down to help them dry out. By mid-afternoon, the curd is ready for the next part of the process. It is put through a mill that looks like a small mangle. Like much else at Smart's, this has little to do with modern technology – the mill itself is Victorian. This mixes the

curd thoroughly, and at this stage salt is added, which reacts with the lactic acid to stop the process developing. Now it is ready to be put into moulds ready for the presses. Like the mill, these are far from new. They all work on the same basic mechanical system of screws, weights and levers to exert a pressure of about a ton. They are rather splendid cast-iron machines. One of them, made by Thomas Cobbett, has cast into its frame the information that it has won first prize at various exhibitions from London to Amsterdam. It does not say when, but a good guess would be that it was sometime in the late 19th century. Here the cheeses will stay for a couple of days

before being taken away to the store, where they will be left to mature, in the case of Double Gloucester for at least six months. During all this time, the flavour is developing to the full richness one associates with Double Gloucester or to the gentler taste and softer texture of the Single.

Smart's farmhouse cheeses is an impressive success story. But it is not just the making of cheese that makes the operation profitable. The family sell their cheese direct to the customers, both visitors to the farm and online via their website. They are also regular stallholders at local farmers' markets, which have proved a godsend to many small producers. It is a story that is still developing. There are plans to increase production by making a blue cheese. This will involve a certain amount of building work, as the present building has reached capacity. The results should be, at the very least, interesting and could lead to a whole new and exciting range of Gloucester cheeses. If the new cheese is as good as the old, it will be worth waiting for.

Cheese making is just one way in which a valuable foodstuff can be preserved, which was essential in the days before refrigeration. The bacon produced from the Old Spot pigs serves the same purpose. The other popular method of preservation that has survived into the present day is smoking. *CB*

Mrs Smart packing Double Gloucester cheese
ready for sale in the farm shop.

The
Smoke House

The east coast of Britain, from Scotland right down to East Anglia, was once famous for its herring fishing. The fleets would follow the shoals in their travels and by the late 19th century, the catches were immense: in the 1880s over a million pounds in weight (about 450 tons) of the fish were being landed every year. The problem was that there was far more being landed than could be used on the spot and instantly. The answer was to preserve them by smoking: the herring would be transformed into the kipper.

In 1872 William Fortune established a smoke house in Whitby under the shadow of the cliffs, and it has been run by the same family ever since. This is not a new establishment for me. I was about 11 years old when my family came here for a holiday. My friend and I must have got bored and run out of money for the amusement arcades, so we wandered off to see if there was anything interesting to find: we found Fortune's. It remains a vivid memory, with its shiny black, tarry walls and the powerful smells of wood smoke and fish. Everyone was very kind to the two small boys and allowed us to help hang up the fish. We were delighted with the adventure, our parents rather less enchanted. We must have stunk the place out as our clothes were liberally daubed with fish scales and tar. I cannot remember anything else much from the holiday, but I've never forgotten Fortune's, so there was a worry: would it have changed completely, been modernised and sanitised? I needn't have fretted: it was just as I remembered it from all those years ago.

Nowadays, the herring are frozen on board as soon as they are caught, so they arrive at the smoke house in prime condition. They are then slit open and degutted, a job that Barry and David Fortune can do in a matter of seconds. After this the fish are soaked in brine for around 40 minutes to enhance the flavour. They are then hung up on poles, so that during the smoking process any moisture can drip out. It is the nature of the smoke

Above: Fortune's sign on their Whitby shop.

Opposite: The herring have been split open and are now being hung on poles ready to be taken to the smoke house.

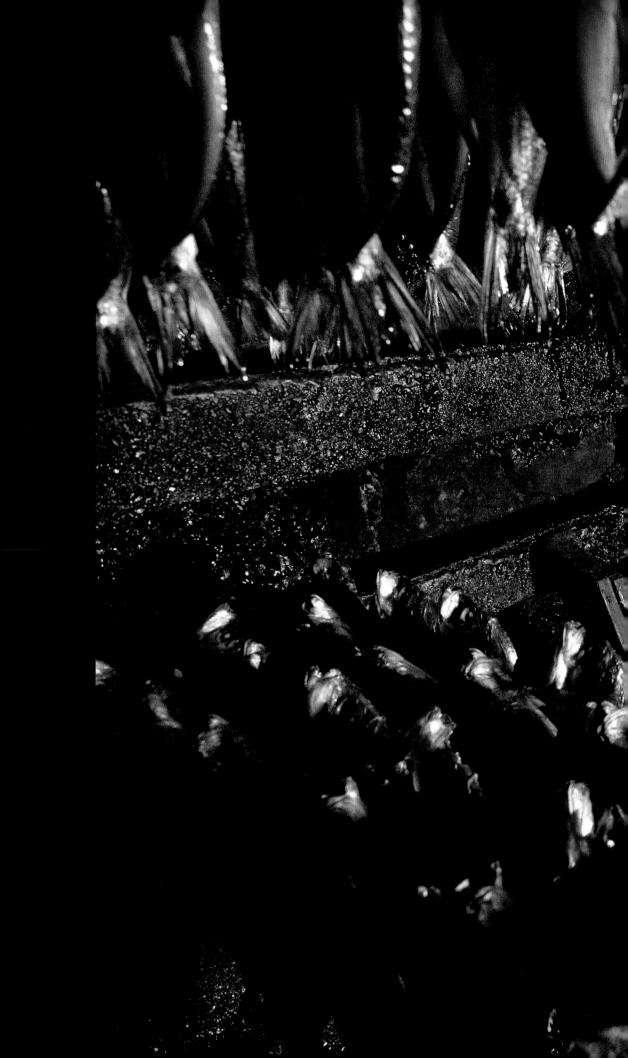

Herring being hung up in the smoke house;
the walls blackened by over a century of use.

Above: The modest shop where the kippers are sold has scarcely changed over the years.

Left: Lighting the fire that consists mainly of oak shavings, with a little beech and soft wood.

A fresh supply of kippers being delivered to the shop.

that gives the kipper its unique flavour. The fires are lit using mainly oak shavings together with beech and some soft wood. This has to be a gentle smouldering rather than a blazing fire with leaping flames. Altogether, the smoking process lasts for 18 hours, after which the kippers can be boxed up and sent away or taken down the road to the family shop. There is never any shortage of customers. There are many candidates for a traditional British breakfast, from porridge in Scotland to the heart-attack special with bacon, eggs, black pudding, beans, sausages and anything else that can be got on the plate. But for real, deep flavour there is really nothing to match a good kipper. *CB*

Setting the Table

The
Silversmith

Once you have something ready to be eaten, you need something to eat it with and something on which to put it. For centuries, even the most sophisticated had nothing very much more elaborate for getting food from the table into their mouths than a knife and fingers. A wooden platter or slightly grander pewter might serve for plates. Most of us today of course have cupboards stocked with some form of pottery – cups, plates and bowls – and drawers full of cutlery. This can be comparatively cheap and crude, or grand and expensive. We're going to start with the grandest and most expensive items, silver cutlery – at least, that's what I called it until I learned better when I went to Sheffield.

They say a rich person is born with a silver spoon in their mouth. If it's a new, hand-forged silver spoon then it will almost certainly have been made by Fletcher Robinson Ltd of Sheffield. They are probably the last company in the world specialising in this type of ware, though cutlery is only part of their business. Their speciality is flatware. In the trade the name 'cutlery' refers only to knives: spoons and forks are flatware. What distinguishes their work is that every single piece is hand-made by master craftsmen who have served at least five years' apprenticeship. Watching them at work, one can see why this has to be so: everything relies on personal experience, judgement and immense skill. The easiest way to explain this is to follow the story of a single, apparently simple object – a dessert spoon.

The starting point is the silver itself. This is not the pure metal; that is too soft to be useful. Other elements have to be added to give it strength and hardness, and the metal used here is sterling silver, which contains a minimum of 92.5% pure silver. It arrives in coils, and the first job is to cut a suitable length, known as a slit, that will be exactly right for that particular spoon. For a dessert spoon of a particular pattern, the weight is already known, measured in troy ounces. This is a system of weighing that goes right back to Roman times and, unlike the old Imperial measure, there are 12 troy ounces to the troy pound instead of 16. The troy ounce is equivalent to approximately 31.1 grams, as opposed to 28.4 grams for the more familiar unit. A scale shows the length the slit needs to be cut to to make the spoon of that weight, and it is sliced off in the guillotine. Now work can begin to transform it into a spoon.

Dies that are used for shaping the bowls of fluted silver spoons.

The initial stage of shaping a spoon or fork involves skilful hammering on the anvil.

Bowling: the spoon bowl is shaped by using a drop hammer and dies.

The metal has to be heated and slowly cooled – annealed – to harden it, and then it can be hammered into shape. It is quite extraordinary to see a man with forearms about the size of my legs working with immense speed and power yet with great accuracy and delicacy, constantly turning and moving the metal on the anvil to shape and harden it. During the process, the annealing might be done half a dozen times, and again the matter of judging when it is right for working all comes down to a good eye and years of experience. There is more involved than just hammering out a flat shape: there are subtle variations in the thickness of the silver, which will be thicker near the lip, the area that gets the most wear. This is one of the characteristics of hand-forged silver that cannot be duplicated in machine-made items. The result is a flat, spoon-shaped blank.

The next process is 'bowling', which is, as you would expect, shaping the bowl of the spoon. This is carried out using a massive drop hammer. Depending on the design to be used, a head will be selected for the hammer. The space beneath the hammerhead is filled with molten tin. The hammer is dropped, gently at first, then with increasing force to create a mould. The spoon blank is then placed above the mould and the hammer again banged fairly gently onto the blank, forcing it into the appropriate bowl shape. The hammer is now allowed its full drop and the building shakes with every blow.

From here the spoon goes for filing, an operation that involves far more than simply getting rid of rough edges. The spoon handle will need to be bent in a curve specific to the particular design. Each design has a master pattern made of copper, against which the silver spoon will be measured.

The fork is flat when it reaches the filer, who has to bend it to just the right shape.

The piece of silver on the left is exactly the right amount needed to make the spoon on the right.

Weighing finished ware for assaying.

The spoon is held over a shaped block placed in a vice, and hammered into shape with a lead hammer. Lead is used because it is softer than the silver, so can be used for shaping without damaging the surface. Inevitably, the lead gets distorted and worn, in which case it is simply taken away, melted and reformed as a new head. Filing is another highly skilled job, which involves seeing the spoon as a three-dimensional object, in which the handle and bowl have to be perfectly aligned, while at the same time the bend of the handle must be identical for every spoon in a set, so that they nest comfortably together. Everything depends on the eye of the master craftsman and his skill with the hammer. Watching him at work, it is easy to see why such a long apprenticeship is needed: skills like this are not easily learned. Some of us suspect we would never master them.

The spoon has achieved its final shape, but it has to be given that shimmering gleam by being buffed on a series of wheels to produce the perfect finish. The spoon still has to be treated with care: even at this late stage it could be ruined. The finished product is stamped with the name of the retailer. Looking through old ledgers from the 1930s, many well-known names come up, such as Mappin & Webb, who had ordered two dozen coffee spoons at a cost of £2. 3s. So their name would go on the spoons, which would be sent to London for assaying and given the London assay mark.

The customer could well think that his spoons had actually been made in the capital, not in Sheffield. Today everything goes to the Sheffield assay office. For assaying purposes the finished products have to be reweighed – some of the silver will be lost in filing and finishing – but the precious dust isn't thrown away, it's carefully collected for reuse.

There are other processes that can be used for providing different shapes. There is a huge selection of dies for different patterns. These can be used with a massive press, originally operated in a mint for making coins. This can be used to give a variety of exotic shapes – for example, to spoon handles. One of the great features of Fletcher Robinson is that they are almost infinitely adaptable, able to produce one-off pieces as well as large runs of standard designs. They have recently been working to produce silver versions of David Mellor designs, reproducing in silver what he made in stainless steel. These are modern classics.

Fletcher Robinson stands at the end of a very, very long tradition of Sheffield silversmiths that can be traced right back to Nicholas Bartholomew in the middle of the 16th century. The skills were passed down from craftsman to apprentice through the generations until the early 19th century, when the company Francis Higgins and Sons was set up. In 1898, one of the partners took over and it became W. H. Brewis

The company holds a wide range of dies of different shapes
and sizes for their cutlery and flatware.

& Co. The first Fletcher appears early in the 20th century with the
formation of C. W. Fletcher (Silversmiths). Throughout all this time,
very little changed: had Nicholas Bartholomew returned at the start of
the 21st century, he would soon have fitted into the working practices.
Nevertheless, it seemed to many that hand forging was a thing of the
past in the machine age, and there was a very real possibility that the
chain would be broken. Fortunately, there was one very important customer over in New York, James Robinson. He valued the unique ware,
and rather than see it disappear, he bought the company in 2002, with

very clear intentions. All too often takeovers involve scrapping the old,
regardless of its worth, and putting in something considered more modern – and cheaper to run. Not James Robinson: he wanted everything
kept just as it was, producing goods of a quality that was unobtainable
by any other means. There are other companies capable of hand forging,
but there may be just one left that uses this technique and nothing else.
That company is Fletcher Robinson: long may it continue, and let us hope
that a new generation will, in time, learn the old skills that are needed to
produce silverware of this quality. *CB*

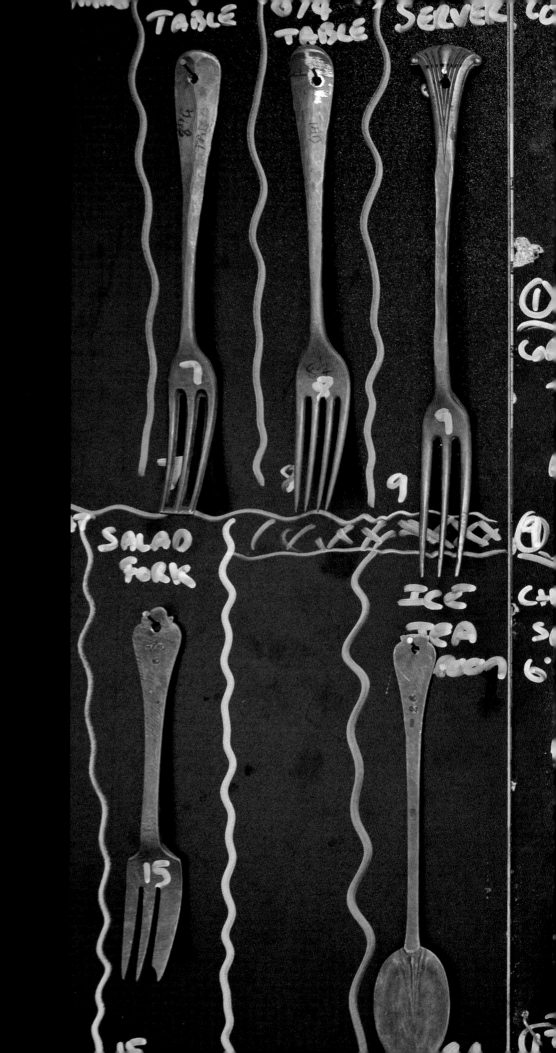

A selection of standard patterns against which
the new ware can be measured.

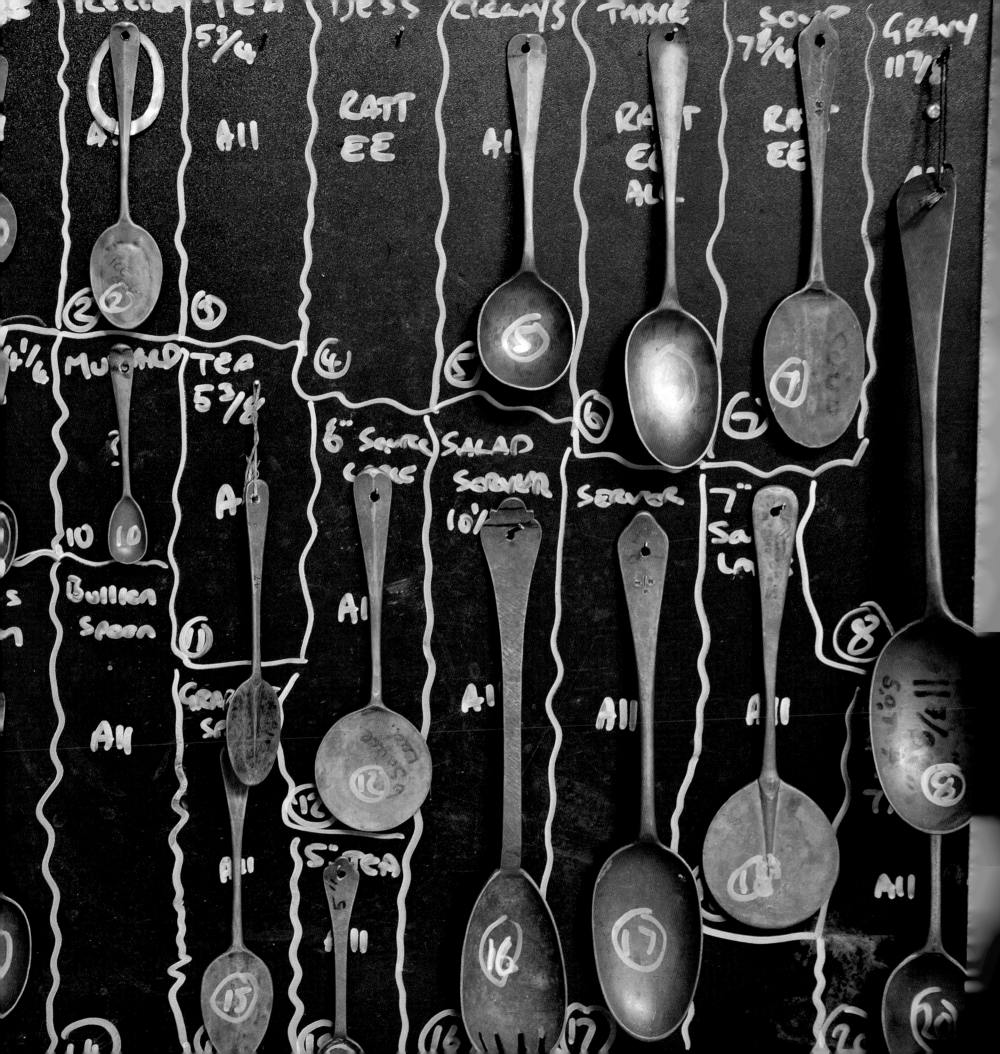

The Pottery

No one can be certain how long pots have been made in the area in and around Stoke-on-Trent, but there is ample evidence that as an industry it was sending out ware to the rest of Britain as long ago as the 17th century. It developed in this area simply because all the necessary elements were found here: suitable clay for making fireproof bricks with which to build the kilns and coal to fire them and, of course, the clay itself from which the pots would be made. The only problem was that the clay was quite dark: if you wanted a snowy white plate or cup, then it had to be covered in a heavy glaze. There were great changes made in the 18th century that were to make Staffordshire pottery acceptable to aristocratic taste and popular with an increasingly affluent middle class. One of the leaders of the movement was Josiah Wedgwood. He made use of an established technique, incorporating ground flint into the clay, which lightened the colour during firing, and imported lighter-coloured clays from Devon and Cornwall. He became the chief promoter of the Trent & Mersey Canal, which meant that the raw materials could easily be brought to the works – clay shipped round the coast to Liverpool and flint from East Anglia brought along the Trent. There was another innovation, actually developed in Liverpool – transfer printing – that made it easier to produce elaborate designs on an industrial scale. All these changes can be seen at the Burleigh Pottery.

The business began back in the middle of the 19th century, and by 1889 it had moved to a factory that was regarded as a model of modernity, the Middleport Pottery in Burslem. You might expect such an important works to be situated on the main road, but instead you turn off down a series of narrow streets lined by small terraced houses. The main building is typical of a 19th-century pot works: a long brick range with a single high, wide entrance to take carts in and out under the eye of the management in the office at the gate. Once you are inside, the odd location makes complete sense: the pottery might not be on a main road, but it was built on the most important transport route, the canal, and it still has a large wharf with two cranes, though these are no longer in use. Here too is one of the traditional bottle ovens, a shapely structure in which the ware was once fired. It is altogether elegant, but there was nothing elegant about the smoke that erupted from this and other kilns, often leaving Stoke darkened under man-made clouds.

Even today no one has found a better way of carrying fragile ware around the works than by carrying it on wooden boards.

The operative is holding up a 'pancake' of clay, which he
will slap down onto the mould spinning on the turntable
to form a plate.

Above: Checking the 'slip', the creamy mixture of clay and water which will be pumped to the upper floor for use in casting ware.

Right: Dipping the ware in the glazing mixture: the pink colour will disappear during firing, leaving a transparent glaze.

No one mourns the fact that it is no longer in use, but many are pleased that it has survived, even if the five other kilns that were once part of the works have gone. So, there have been great changes, but when we come to look at the actual manufacturing processes, what is amazing is just how many traditional ideas and technologies have survived.

The processes start with the raw ingredients, which are much as they were in Wedgwood's time – clay from the West Country and powdered flint. These have to be carefully mixed with water in just the right proportions in a blunger – a great cast-iron tank – and stirred by rotating blades. The process has to be continued for many hours, before the mixture,

known as 'slip', about the consistency of double cream, is run off into tanks under the floor. From here it can be pumped up to workshops for casting. Not all the clay used has this liquid consistency: some is used in more solid form. This has to go through separate processing. First the slip is taken to a press, in this case in a nearby mill, where it is pumped between plates and then squeezed so that the moisture gradually drips out, leaving cakes of clay. To ensure all air bubbles are removed it has to be mixed once more in the pug mill, from which the clay emerges as an elongated cylinder. Most of the machinery in the slip room is run from overhead shafts with rotating cams to work the pumps that date back to the time when power was

Top: One half of a mould that will be used for casting a teapot.

Above: A pierced bowl: all the incisions have to be made by hand –
one of the many skilled tasks perfected by the pottery workers.

Creating plaster moulds that will be used for casting
different types of ware.

Printing a pattern onto tissue paper that will then be transferred onto the ware.

Left: A section of the printed paper is being removed that that will then be applied to the cup on the bench.

Below: The finished product.

supplied by a steam engine. And this venerable machine, a simple single-cylinder engine, has survived, even if it no longer does the work, which has been handed over to an electric motor.

There are two paths to follow, starting with the slip. Casting involves making the original pot, a jug or teapot for example, and using that to create a plaster mould. The actual moulds into which the slip is poured don't last for more than a few castings before they have to be replaced with new moulds made from the master case. So the first step in the process involves taking out the correct case – and there are literally thousands of moulds and cases held in the company store, itself the most complete collection to be found anywhere, many items dating back well into the 19th century. The mould maker mixes plaster and fastens the two parts of the case together with a cat's cradle of string. He will normally make several different moulds at the same time. Once the plaster is ready, it has to be poured quickly into the cases, before it starts to set. Once the plaster has hardened, the cases are unwrapped and the new moulds set aside to dry. Like so much of the work here, it looks deceptively simple, but actually requires considerable skill. A mould is rather like

a negative in a photographic studio: with a negative, what is black will come out white, and vice versa; with the mould, what is blank will become solid.

The actual casting of the object, for example a teapot, starts with pouring the slip into the mould, filling all the teapot-shaped gaps. The plaster absorbs some of the moisture and the clay gradually hardens until, at the right moment, the mould is broken open, leaving a version of the teapot in hardened clay. It will not be perfect: the spout will have a ragged end and there will be a line of raised clay where the two parts of the mould met. To remove the blemishes, the pot is passed on for sponging and fettling. A damp sponge can be used to smooth over rough parts, and the ridges and blemishes are removed with a scalpel-like knife. It is now ready to be moved on to the next stage. The method of moving pots around the works is unchanged from Victorian times, simply because no one has found a more efficient way of doing it. They are carried on ware boards. These are made of very light wood. The ware is lined up on top, the board is hoisted onto a shoulder, and away it goes. One wonders how many pots got broken by newcomers before they mastered the technique.

An old sign at Middleton Pottery, showing changing ownership over the years.

The frontage at Middleton is typical of Stoke pot banks, with its single wide waggon entrance.

Not all ware is cast: plates and bowls are pressed. That long sausage of clay from the pug mill is brought up to the workplace and sliced into a series of roundels. In a remarkably speedy operation, the clay roundel is picked up and thrown down onto the centre of a spinning dish that turns the thick roll into a thin pancake. A mould is put upside down on another disc and the pancake slapped down on top of it. The clay takes the shape of the mould, the edges are trimmed, the mould and newly formed plate are stacked up on one side to dry, and the process begins all over again. Again, this sounds straightforward, but if the operative doesn't hit the centre every time, the clay spins off in a wobbling mess. Making a bowl is slightly more complex, as it involves working the clay up the sides of a spinning former, much closer to the traditional art of the potter. The items are now taken to one of the kilns for firing, and when they emerge the pots will now be known as biscuit. The clay will have changed colour to a pure white.

Whatever the ware, plate, cup, saucer or jug, it is now ready to have the decoration applied. Transfer printing has scarcely changed since the 18th century and the patterns that are used are all completely traditional. The company has a large store of beautiful engraved cylinders, each with its own attractive pattern. The process starts rather like any other form of printing, with the etched roller being inked with coloured ink and then rolled over the paper. But here the paper is tissue-thin – surprisingly it is paper originally made for French cigarettes. It takes the imprint, which remains very sticky on it. Each individual tissue is passed onto the conveyor belt, which is rather more like a moving washing line, over which the papers are draped. They are moved on to a series of desks where the decoration is applied. In some cases it is applied all over, but for others where only some parts are decorated, such as the rim of a cup, the tissue has to be sliced into sections. Whichever method is being used, the work all depends on a keen eye and a steady hand. Once the tissue has been rubbed onto the piece, there is no way of correcting a fault. Before the next stage, the tissue has to be removed. Because the ink is oil based, it can be washed off with water.

The final stage is glazing. The material of the transparent glaze is coloured pink with vegetable dye. This will lose its colour on the firing, but it makes it easy to see if the entire piece is covered before it is passed on. The glaze is dried by passing it slowly through a heated tunnel. Now it is ready for the final stage – to be taken to the glost oven, the glaze kiln, for the last firing. What emerges is a beautifully shaped piece of ware, with an attractive coloured pattern laid over a white base. This is the sort of ware our Victorian ancestors prized, and it is admired just as much today as it was then. Burleigh ware is distinctive, traditional and expertly crafted. It represents a remarkable continuity of ideas and practices that have lasted for more than a century and a half, and there seems to be no good reason why they should not continue for a long time to come. *CB*

The old bottle kiln that was once used for firing ware: the last bottle kiln firing in Stoke took place in 1976.

Two Pints and a Dram

The Maltings

Britain has three traditional alcoholic drinks, and two of them, beer and whisky, start with the same basic ingredient – malted barley – so it seems logical to begin this section at Britain's oldest working maltings at Warminster.

The best barley is grown in thin soil overlying a foundation of chalk, and if you look at a geological map of Britain, you'll see a chalk band that runs from the Wash on the east coast all the way down to the south coast at Dorset; and there at the western edge in Wiltshire sits Warminster. There's no chalk to the west of there, so for brewers in Somerset, Devon and Cornwall, Warminster was the first stop if they wanted first-class malt. That explains why, in the middle of the 19th century, there were 36 maltings in the town. It was at this time that William Morgan, described in official documents as a 'common brewer', bought a house in Pound Street and began its conversion to a malt house, gradually extending the buildings over the years. As his business grew, his competitors foundered, and today this is the only malting left in the town.

The basic process of malting is simple in its essentials – though a lot more complex and sophisticated in practice. The dried barley is delivered from the farm and then needs to be soaked to increase the water content to the point where the grain comes back to life and can begin germinating. The germination is allowed to continue to the point where the starch in the grain has been converted into sugar, and then the process is stopped by heating in a kiln. After that the barley has become malt.

This story is not just about an industrial process: it is also the story of the barley itself. A key figure is the splendidly named Edwin Sloper Beaven, whose background was in farming, but who had studied chemistry at Framlingham College, Suffolk. He joined Morgan in the business and was to marry the boss's daughter. He found himself in a position where all his skills came together: he knew farming practices at first hand, read widely in the sciences, and from Morgan had learned all the intricacies of malting. When he eventually took over the business, he was determined to improve his basic raw material. Barley was grown in many different varieties with varied characteristics, and what Beaven wanted was to find a grain that could be grown consistently and had all the best characteristics.

'Ploughing' the germinating barley on one of the malting floors at Warminster Maltings – the grain has to be turned on a regular basis.

At the appropriate moment, the grain is dropped down from the malting floor into the kiln, where it will be heated to prevent further germination.

Opposite: The barley has been soaked in water and is now being spread out on the malting floor to begin germination.

After years of experimental testing he produced what he considered the ideal. It was called Plumage Archer, because it was a hybrid of the English Archer grain and Plumage from Sweden. It was a huge success and helped establish Warminster Maltings as one of the finest in the land – and also led to a long association with Guinness. Farmers found the new grain increased their yields, maltings found it worked perfectly – and brewers discovered it made brilliant beer. For 40 years Plumage Archer was everyone's favourite malt.

It was inevitable that eventually someone would come up with a better alternative after such a long time, and the man who did was Dr. G. D. H. Bell of Cambridge, who developed the variety known as Maris Otter, which is the variety used at Warminster Maltings today.

The maltings were owned for a time by Guinness but were bought by the present owner Robin Appel in 2001. Since then he has lovingly cared for the buildings, restoring them where necessary but always with a view to keeping the glorious tradition intact. He was our guide when we toured the maltings, and his enthusiasm kept rising to the surface like the head on a fine pint. There are very few maltings left that still use the old methods that are practised here, but Robin was adamant that his use of them has nothing to do with sentimentality. He is convinced that this is the way to get the best possible product. He is equally convinced that Maris Otter, which had begun to lose its popularity, is still the finest barley in the world for malting and when he took over he was determined to preserve it for posterity – and he's succeeded.

We started outside with a very ordinary metal bin into which trucks from the farms tip their loads of barley. These days, instead of a sack hoist, the grain is moved into the building by an efficient auger, which is not exactly a modern invention: it's also known as the Archimedes screw, named after the man who invented it over two thousand years ago. The grain arrives from all over the country. Recent years have seen a huge increase in small breweries and microbreweries and many of them, as well as setting high standards, also want to be able to claim a local connection. So a brewery in Shropshire will send down grain grown in the county so that it can proudly claim the home-grown nature of its ale.

Inside, the first stage in the process takes us back to the 19th century. The grain is fed into the steeps, immense cast-iron, flat-bottomed, rectangular tanks. These were designed for the convenience of the tax assessors rather than the maltsters when installed in the 19th century. The excise men calculated their tax on volumes of grain – and with tanks like these all you needed was a tape measure and simple arithmetic. The grain is then covered in water, drawn up from a well in the heart of the complex. It will remain in

there for about three days, during which time its water content will increase from around 13 to 45 per cent. It is now ready to start germinating.

Once the tank has been drained, the grain has to be removed, and again an auger is used. If it hadn't been for the customs officials, life could have been made a lot easier by the use of a downward-curving bottom to the tank, so that the grain would slide to the lowest point, where it could be picked up. Instead, in the early hours of the morning, the men have to climb in and shovel the grain to the centre of the tank, where it can be collected. The next stage is the very heart of the operation and the part that distinguishes this type of malting from the modern, computer-controlled process followed in other parts of the country. It is the operation that gives it its name – a floor malting.

The grain is spread over two floors, one above the other, in long rooms with shuttered openings all down their length: the shutters are closed in winter to keep in the warmth and opened in summer to let it out. It is spread evenly to a depth of between 3 and 12 inches depending on the time of year. It is here that the barley begins the process of germination, but it has to be carefully tended day and night. It is regularly turned, by ploughing. This involves dragging an implement that looks like an oversized three-pronged fork through the grain. Not immediately obvious are the downward-pointing triangular metal blades at the end of each prong that actually turn the barley. The process allows all the grain to get a good supply of oxygen, releases carbon dioxide and, as the process develops, prevents the little growing rootlets from getting tangled. Just like conventional ploughing out in the fields, the result is a series of ridges and furrows, but instead of a muddy brown, these are a rich field of gold. Sometimes, if the weather is particularly warm, a machine very like a lawnmower is used, whose spinning

Above: Warminster Maltings have occupied this site since the middle of the 19th century.
Right: Malted barley, bagged up and ready to be sent off to the brewery.
Opposite: The painted sign over the office door shows the original owner.

blades throw the grain high into the air as they turn.

The grain is not only turned at roughly three-hourly intervals for five to six days, it is also inspected to check its development. This calls for expert judgement, assessing both the appearance and feel of the grain, the sort of skill that only comes from long experience. This reliance on the human touch is also one of the distinguishing features of a floor malting that differentiates it from modern, computer-controlled maltings. As Robin Appel explained, they do not work to a set of predetermined rules: 'Because barley is a natural being and each batch that comes in has come from a different field and has different elements – it's going to express itself differently.' The expert maltster will know just the right moment to stop the germination process, when all the starch in the grain has been converted to sugar, and green shoots have not yet begun to appear. When that moment comes, the barley is moved on to the kiln.

Originally, the kilns were heated by coal fires – the old fire doors are still there – which would have been tended to day and night by men working in shifts. Today, a less labour-intensive gas-heated kiln is used. The intense heat stops the process of germination and the barley has been turned into malt. Now all that remains is to put it through a screening process, using a machine not unlike the bolter of a flour mill. This removes the rootlets, now reduced to a powder by the heat of the kiln. This isn't waste: known as 'malt culms', it is used for cattle feed.

Different batches of malt are earmarked for different breweries. They are kept in great bins until the day before delivery, when they're packed up and despatched. There is one department at the maltings that would not

have been there in the old days: the laboratory. This is used to test the barley when it arrives. A hundred grains are chosen and allowed to germinate under controlled conditions – if too many fail, the batch is rejected. Then, at the end of processing, the malt itself is tested. Nitrogen content is measured and the malt is, in effect, brewed on a very small scale to make sure it produces wort that will be acceptable to the brewer. The brewer knows that he is getting a traditionally crafted malt of the very best quality, ideally suited to the type of beer he intends to make. The malt can be sent anywhere. I have a local pub, the Village Inn in Nailsworth, Gloucestershire, with its own small brew house that has only been in operation for a few years. It gets its malt from Warminster and I can certainly vouch for the end product. The maltings also supply far larger breweries, and the next visit will be to one of these, where tradition rules just as it does at Warminster Maltings. *CB*

The Brewery

Brewing changed dramatically in the second half of the 20th century. Centralisation, take-overs and closures led to an inevitable loss of variety, but worse was to follow. The big brewers discovered the delights of keg beer, which for them had the great advantages of being easy to keep, always looking clear and having what they considered an attractive sparkle: more of that later. In the process, however, many drinkers were convinced that flavour had been sacrificed for convenience, and as a result a pressure group was formed to try and stem the sparkly tide: the Campaign for Real Ale, CAMRA. It was hugely successful and real ale – that too will be defined later – is now available again in the majority of pubs, where once it had to be hunted down with all the enthusiasm of a pig sniffing out truffles. Perhaps some of the smaller breweries would have survived without CAMRA's help, but that is by no means certain. So what do traditional breweries do that makes them special? To understand what it is requires a brief note on how beer is actually made.

Brewing of most beers is basically a very simple process, only requiring four basic ingredients: malt, yeast, hops and water. The process essentially consists of extracting the sugars from the malt with hot water, then boiling with hops and fermenting with yeast, to make alcohol. The quality of the beer depends on any number of factors. The first is the quality of the products. We've just seen the process that provides what many think is the very best malt. The character of the water plays a crucial role. One reason why Burton upon Trent became such a popular place with brewers was the nature of the water, obtained from local wells – and very definitely not

Above: Dray horses are still used for local deliveries from the Hook Norton brewery.

Left: Malted barley being dropped down a copper tube into the mash tun, where it will be heated with water to extract the sugars.

Left: Hook Norton is a typical tower brewery: the timbered structure is a covered sack hoist that takes the malt to the top to start the processes.

Below left: Sacks of malt being unloaded at the top of the tower.

from the river Trent. The hops enable beer to be kept longer before going sour and also give beers their distinctive flavours. Traditionally the hops have come from Kent and Worcester, and have wonderful names, such as Fuggles and Goldings. Cheaper alternatives are available from mainland Europe, but many brewers feel the results are never as satisfactory. One head brewer I know resigned in protest when a new management team insisted he bought cheaper hops – and went off to found his own brewery. The brewery that listened to an accountant rather than their brewer has since closed, after going into administration. The brewer who went off on his own is thriving. There would appear to be a moral to this story.

You might think that yeast is yeast, and that there is not much more one can say about it, but different strains have different characteristics: those used for brewing beer are traditionally different from those used for making lager. One other ingredient is often added, known as finings, generally in the form of isinglass. This was originally made from the swim bladder of the sturgeon, but cod and other fish were later substituted. Quite how anyone hit on the idea of adding such an unlikely ingredient to beer is a mystery, but it does a very useful job in clearing away any cloudiness from the beer. Strict vegetarians have been known to refuse to drink beer because of this fishy addition.

Those are the general principles, but how does this translate into the workings of a brewery? There are few better places to go to find an answer than the little village of Hook Norton in Oxfordshire. In 1849 John Hams began brewing in his farmhouse, which proved a very successful venture and the Hook Norton brewery was born. Moving onto a large-scale commercial footing called for a purpose-built brewery, fitted out with all the very latest equipment. That was in 1892, and fundamentally that is the brewery still in use today. The family opted for a tower brewery, which is just what its name suggests. The idea is beautifully simple. Beer making involves a succession of different processes, so it makes sense to take all the basic ingredients up to the top of the tower, and let everything else happen with the aid of that always-available, free-of-charge power source, gravity. But you are going to need help getting everything up to the top in the first place, and the first thing you see when you walk inside is the 1892 solution to that problem: the steam engine.

HM Revenue and Customs have a legal right to access all parts of the brewery, so a set of keys is always available.

Above: Testing the alcohol content of the liquor in the fermentation vessel.

Left: The milling machine at the top of the tower is used for crushing the barley.

The company went to the geographical heart of the brewing industry when they ordered their new equipment – and this steam engine, specially developed for brewery work, was supplied by Buxton & Thornley of Burton upon Trent. Steam enthusiasts might like to know that it is a single-cylinder horizontal engine and should be delighted to hear that it is still in use, not as a museum exhibit, but as part of the working life of the brewery. Originally, it was used for two types of work: operating the sack hoist and other machinery, and pumping water. The brewery had its own well, and the old pumps are still there, but the well became silted and new bore holes had to be dug and different pumps used. It is still the same

spring – just coming up from different holes in the ground. The water is one of the ingredients that give the beer its character, except that brewers never call it water. It is liquor, and remains liquor throughout its various transformations before becoming beer.

One of the delights of this brewery is the wonderful ingenuity combined with the simple mechanical devices found everywhere. Here in the engine room is a gauge showing liquor levels. No one wants to stomp up to the top of the tower every time they want to check on water levels in the tanks, so they devised a simple system of floats attached to wires that reach right down to the ground floor, where the indicator board shows the levels in gallons via a pointer at the end of the wire. The world may have gone metric, but the brewery has stayed loyal to older measures – even temperature is still measured in Fahrenheit.

The raw ingredients are taken to the top of the tower, so that is the logical starting place for a description of how the brewery works. It is a good long climb up old iron staircases to reach the cast-iron cold-water tanks, also supplied by Buxton & Thornley. These are themselves a testament to how well the building was constructed. Once full of liquor, they weigh a colossal 60 tons – we're staying with the brewers and ignoring metrication. At the next level down is the grain mill. The 'modern' milling machine that has taken over from earlier grindstones has only been here 110 years. The barley is passed through rollers to emerge as grist – everything, of course, is grist to the mill. From here it passes into a hopper, ready to continue its journey.

The barley is passed down into one of a pair of mash tuns, rather like gargantuan barrels with hinged lids. This is done through a large copper

Checking the contents of a mash tun.

tube, which can be placed over either of the tuns by turning a handle that operates a surprisingly complex set of gears. This is another of those Victorian mechanisms that are so appealing, not least because it is possible to see through the complexity to an essentially very basic idea. Here the barley is mashed – heated with the liquor to extract the sugars. At the end of the process it is still liquor, but instead of merely being water it is now 'wort', and it continues down to the next floor and the coppers, where it is boiled with hops. Here they tend to use three main varieties, all grown in Worcestershire. They not only give flavour, they also remove some of the proteins that have been released, which would otherwise prevent the beer from clearing.

Now the hops have to be removed and the wort has to be cooled. Originally, this involved more pumping, right up to the top of the tower, where it was poured into an immense shallow tank. Louvred windows on all four walls were opened up and the cool breezes did the rest. It worked very well, but was not exactly hygienic. Modern heat exchangers do the job today.

Now the liquor continues its journey to the exciting bit – the fermentation vessels, where the yeast has been added and starts to create alcohol. A thick foam forms and the air has a sharp tang as carbon dioxide is released: sticking your head over a vessel is a good way to clear sinus problems, but don't keep it there for long. To keep the yeast well oxygenated, it is regularly stirred.

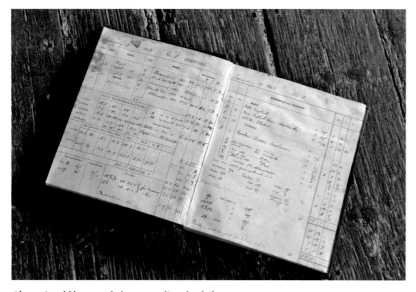

Above: An old brewery ledger recording the daily output.

Opposite: There is only one way to clean out a mash tun – get inside and do it by hand.

Brewers obviously love having their own language, because the device used is known by the intriguing name of 'rousing pole'. Periodically, the froth is drained away through a large funnel and kept to preserve the yeast strain for another day.

Once fermentation is complete, we have finally arrived at liquor that can be called beer. It is ready now to be sent on one last drop to tanks from which the casks are filled. Before the cask is closed, a small plug of hops is dropped into each one, for that little extra bit of flavour. That is not quite the end of the story, for some natural secondary fermentation continues in the cask: hence cask-conditioned beers. This is what makes real ale special. Keg beers are pasteurised for preservation, and given a lift by pumping in carbon dioxide. To the real-ale enthusiast, the pasteurised beers are gassy and unpleasant on the tongue; to others, the cask-conditioned ales are old-fashioned examples of the warm, flat beer that was acceptable once but has no place in the modern world. They will probably never agree, but the reader will not have too much trouble working out which side of the fence the author and the photographer have set up their bar stools.

After an appropriate time, the casks are ready to be sent out to pubs around the country. At Hook Norton, the local pubs get a very special delivery service. The casks are taken on a dray pulled by a splendid pair of horses. It may not be the most economical way of working, but the horses are valuable publicity aids, regularly appearing at shows. It is not an exercise in nostalgia. This is all part of the process of telling customers that this really is a traditional brewery, where quality and continuity matter. The final proof is in the tasting, and for generations of beer drinkers, the name 'Hooky' has always been a guarantee of a pint worth savouring. ⫚

The
Cider Maker

The essentials of beer brewing are straightforward and involve only a few ingredients, but cider making is even simpler. There is only one ingredient – apples – and the process can be reduced to three stages: pick the apples, squash them to remove the juice, then let the juice ferment. But as any cider lover will tell you, the elements may be simple but the possibilities for subtle variations are endless.

Apple trees are native to Britain, but we have no means of knowing whether or not cider was made in ancient times. What we do know is that the Normans were, and still are, enthusiastic cider makers, and when they invaded Britain and settled down, they brought their own varieties of apples with them – apples suitable for cider making. Written records of early cider making are scarce, but as early as the beginning of the 13th century hogsheads of cider were reported as being sent to the exchequer as tax payments. Rather surprisingly, this first record comes from Norfolk, but today cider making is very much associated with the West Country, and there is no better place to see the process than on a Devon farm.

To see cider-making processes in action, you have to pick your time of year, arriving in autumn when the last of the crop is being picked and the apples are ready for pressing. We visited Brimblecombe's Cider, near Dunsford on the edge of Dartmoor, on just such a cool day at the very end of the season, to find the owners, Ron and Bev Barter, still hard at work filling sacks full of apples. Cider orchards such as these are magical places, which have nothing to do with regimentation and conformity. There is no obvious pattern to the planting of the trees, which have now reached mature old age, and they are not limited to a single variety. The branches were still heavy with fruit, covering every shade from acidic green to bright red. No one really knows when these orchards were first planted, but the names can be found on maps and documents from centuries ago – even New End Orchard was only new a few hundred years ago. There are 20 different species of apple here, and their names are equally redolent of tradition. Who could resist The Fair Maid of Devon? But do you feel quite so well disposed towards Pig's Snout? In fact the latter looks like a sour crab

Packing the cider press with alternate layers of straw and pulped apples.

Not exactly a high tech sign, but very appropriate for a traditional cider maker.

apple, and tastes like it too. The Ten Commandments only reveals its origins when you slice it in half, to expose a neat circle of ten dark marks round the pips. There is less of a problem in working out how Slack Me Girdle got its name – it is apparently a notoriously gassy apple.

The apples are not actually picked, but shaken off the trees. All you need is a fallen branch with a 'v' at the end, like a pitchfork, and you stick it under a branch and push. It is not just that this makes life simple: if the apples fall off then they are ripe and ready for use. If nothing drops, then you have to come back later. Originally the fallen apples were all picked by hand, which is a backbreaking job, but this is one area where mechanisation has taken over, and now they are scooped up by a machine that looks like a cross between a giant vacuum cleaner and a lawnmower. In the season the orchard produces around 20 tons of apples, enough to make 1,500 gallons of cider.

It is a short walk across the fields and through more orchards to the farmhouse and the barn, where cider is made. The barn was actually the farmhouse in Saxon times, but was replaced by something altogether more up to date and modern, though modern is a comparative term here. It happened at some time in the 16th century. The barn is built right up against the hillside, and the apples can be loaded straight into the upper storey, into an area known as The Pound, because this is where apples are pounded into pulp. There is an array of old devices for pulping. Originally, the work would have been done by hand, but that was superseded by the horse mill. All that remains now is the stone circle on the floor, where the apples were placed for crushing by a stone roller. This was fastened to a central pivot, which was rotated by a horse walking endlessly round the circle. The other old machine was obviously thought by its inventor to be a very clever device, so he called it the Ingenio. It is not really that complex: the apples are fed into a hopper and from there they fall in between ribbed rollers worked by a hand crank. Today the job is done much more easily by an electric mill, but this is where modernity ends. The apples are not separated out: it is the mixture of different varieties that gives the cider its complex flavour.

Once the apples have been reduced to pulp they are taken down to the press. This extraordinary device is around 350 years old, constructed out of immense timbers. At the bottom of the machine is a stone trough, and the press itself is lowered down into it by means of a complex set of gears, worked by a capstan on the floor above. First, a layer of pulped apples is placed in the trough, leaving a gap round the perimeter into which the juice can flow. Then a layer of straw is added and tucked round the edges of the pulp, then another layer of pulp, more straw and so on, until the whole stack is about two metres high. Then the press is lowered, slowly compressing the pile. The juice begins to flow and the whole room is perfumed by the scent of ripe apples. At first the work is comparatively easy but as the pile becomes more and more compressed, the capstan becomes increasingly difficult to turn. To extract the very last of the juice, a giant lever is brought into play.

The juice runs from a spout set in the side of the trough into a container

How do you tell if apples are ripe? Shake the tree and any that fall off are ready for use.

Above: The perfect companions: farmhouse cider, bread and cheese.

Left: The apple juice from the press being run off into a barrel, where natural enzymes will start the fermentation process.

Opposite: As the straw and apple layers become more compressed, extra pressure is applied by means of the capstan on the floor above.

in the cellar, the lower floor of the barn. From here it is pumped into fermentation vessels. Unlike brewing, there is no need for any further additives as the apples contain their own supply of wild yeast and the various micro-organisms in the straw help the process along. The juice now remains in the vessels for about six months as the sugars are slowly turned into alcohol. Then the cider is transferred into barrels: some of the wooden barrels have previously held rum, and although they have been thoroughly cleaned, the spirit that still permeates the wood adds its own touch of mellowness to the flavour.

Brimblecombe's cider is, in many ways, a typical Devon farmhouse cider: quite dry but with a real appley flavour. The flavour of any cider depends on a number of factors, most importantly the apples used and how long fermentation continues. The longer the fermentation time the more sugar is converted, and consequently the stronger and drier the cider will be. As with all really interesting, naturally produced drinks, it is the variety of flavours available that distinguishes them from the mass-produced varieties. The same can be said of the other great British drink, from the northern parts of the British Isles – whisky. *CB*

Ron Barter in the lower barn with barrels of slowly maturing cider.

The Distillery

Choosing which Scottish distillery to visit is rather like having to cover the whole subject of French wines from a single vineyard. The first choice was simple: we wanted to go to a distillery famous for its single malts. Most proprietary brands are blends that might contain a mixture of whisky made from malted barley with spirit distilled from other grains. That still left an enormous choice, because malt whiskies come in a rich variety of flavours. The distilleries on Islay, for example, are famous for their very peaty flavour. But we opted for the heartland of Scotch whisky – Speyside and Glenfarclas to be precise. This is a distillery with a long history. The first was recorded here in 1836, but that was just the first legal still: there is more than a strong possibility that distillation went on undiscovered by the Customs and Excise men long before that. It was bought in 1865 by John Grant for £511. 6s. 0d. (about £60,000 today) and it has been owned and run by the Grant family ever since.

Why choose a distillery making just a malt whisky? An easy question to answer: it has a richness and complexity of flavour and each brand is unique. It is a drink to be taken seriously. Some years ago my wife and I were staying in a hotel in Oban and I wandered down to the bar in the evening to be confronted by a grand array of malts. The young lady behind the bar remarked that I was obviously eyeing the selection and I explained that I was looking for something new to try. After some discussion we agreed on a likely candidate. Shortly after another customer appeared, and received the same 'I can see you are eyeing' speech. He was uncertain, so she recommended my particular brand and I agreed enthusiastically with the choice. He ordered it, and then said, 'Could I have it with ginger ale?' The look on the young lady's face was one of unbelieving horror, but she served him anyway, and after he had gone off to find a seat, she exploded: 'If I'd known he was going to do that I'd have given him …' and there you must add the name of whichever popular brand you fancy (or don't fancy). No one should ever do that to a Glenfarclas.

The distillery has been modernised since 1865, with the introduction of such aids as computers to monitor progress, but in their essentials the processes remain just as they were a century and a half ago. It is situated in Strathspey on the edge of the Cairngorms. The hills are an important part

One of the bonded warehouses in which the whisky is stored to slowly mature.

This page and following page: Gleaming copper stills at the Glenfarclas distillery: their basic design has remained unchanged for centuries.

NO.2 SPIRIT STILL
CONTENT
21,200 LITRES

Steaming a barrel to make the wood more pliable.

Fitting metal hoops round the staves to make a watertight barrel at the
Speyside Cooperage.

of the story as the water used in the distillery comes from a spring high up on the slope. It is the purity of the source that is an essential starting point for a successful whisky. There are after all only three ingredients: water, malted barley and yeast.

The first part of the process is exactly the same as that used in brewing beer, apart from the addition of hops. Even the same names, such as 'wort', are used, though water is just water and not liquor. Originally, most distilleries malted their own barley, hence the 'pagoda' roofs of former kilns still to be seen in many locations, but today it is rare. The malt for Glenfarclas comes from maltings in Buckie on the coast between Elgin and Aberdeen. It goes through the same processes as described at Hook Norton and when fermentation is complete, it is passed to the still house. The size of the operation is impressive: 25,000 litres being treated in the next stage.

The liquid that emerges from the first processing stage is low in alcohol. Distillation works because alcohol vaporises more easily than water, so as evaporation begins, it is the lighter spirits that are given off first. The still room itself is dominated by the giant copper stills with their bulbous bases and long, narrowing necks rising from the top and then bending over to the horizontal. The copper is used not because it looks attractive: it acts as a catalyst, helping to purify the spirit and ultimately improving the flavour. These stills are heated directly by gas burners, whose steady roar fills the room. Few distilleries heat directly these days, but here they think it adds to the flavour of the finished product. In the first wash still, there is a small window in the neck of the still, and once liquid can be seen bubbling up there, the temperature is lowered and the distillation process begins. The first distillate, consisting of the low wines, is weak in alcohol and contains impurities, and has to be passed to a second, smaller spirit still. It is now that critical judgements begin to be made.

Not all the distillate is going to be suitable for transforming into whisky. The first part, consisting of the foreshots, contain impurities, including fusil oils – the name 'fusil' actually derives from the German for 'bad liquor'. The liquid flows through a brass casket with glass sides, the spirit safe. This is kept locked to satisfy HMRC that no spirit is being taken away before the duty is paid. After about 20 minutes, the distillate appears as a pure, clear liquid, the middle cut. This is the liquid that will actually be used for whisky, and knowing exactly when to start and end collecting this portion is crucial. The strength can be tested using hygrometers within the safe. The middle cut begins when the alcohol strength is 72

Replacing a worn bung in one of the warehouses.

Inspecting the instruments in the spirit safe to check on the strength and quality of the distillate.

Above: Testing the strength of the whisky with a hygrometer.

Opposite: The matured whisky leaving the distillery for the bottling plant.

per cent and ends when it drops to 60 per cent. The distillation continues, and the next part, consisting of the feints, is collected separately to be mixed with the foreshots and added to the next batch of low wines. Of the 25,000 litres at the beginning of the process, only 4,000 litres actually make up the middle cut, stored in a vat, where they need to be diluted to an acceptable strength.

The next stage sounds simple enough – transfer the contents of the vat to a cask – but there is rather more to it than that. At this stage, the diluted spirit would be drinkable, but would have no character and little flavour. The cask will itself have a major role to play, so it is time for a diversion down Strathspey to Craigellachie and the Speyside Cooperage. This is the last remaining cooperage in Scotland and, like the distillery, it is carrying on a very old tradition.

The cooperage both makes new casks and refurbishes old ones – a barrel is simply one particular size of cask. The story begins over a hundred years before any cask is completed, when an oak tree starts to grow in America. The American oak is particularly prized for its straight trunk and the fineness of the grain. After being felled in America, the timber is cut to appropriate lengths and allowed another year and more to dry out before being shipped to Scotland. The main part of any cask is made up of staves: timbers cut so that they will be concave on the inside of the cask and convex on the outside. These are also cut so that they can be jointed together to make a watertight fit. Raising up a cask is a highly skilled process, starting with two staves being set into a metal hoop as a basis. Then others are selected to complete the round. Once all are in place, a hoop is also placed

on the top, and other hoops added down the barrel to pull it into shape. As these metal hoops are all hammered on by hand, the noise in the workshop is deafening: earplugs are very much the order of the day.

The cask is rolled over to another workshop, where it is covered in a fabric hood and steamed to soften the wood to make it pliable so that the ends can be drawn in. The circular ends – the heads – are made separately. Pieces of oak are cut to different lengths, a long piece for the centre of the head, and decreasing in size towards the rim. It saves timber when the head is cut to a perfect circle.

The most spectacular part of the process is the firing of the inside of the cask: this caramelises the wood and completes the sealing process. Whisky distillers also get their wood toasted, which is when the inside of the barrel is set alight for anything up to 30 seconds, depending on the individual distiller's preference – rather like ordering a steak rare or medium. The heads are set in place, and the final tightening process for the last hoops is left to a hydraulically operated machine to ensure the tightest possible fit. A hose is placed in the bunghole and compressed air sends in a powerful jet of water. If any leaks out, then the cask goes back to the cooper who made it. As all the craftsmen are on piecework, this is bad news. During our visit, none were failed.

Casks can last for decades, but they will need refurbishment from time to time. A second hydraulic machine does the opposite of the first: it pulls the binding hoops away to allow new staves to be added where necessary. The old inner charring will have lost its potency, so that is burned off and the cask toasted again. Including new casks and refurbishments, the

company deals with around 100,000 casks a year. After visiting the cooperage, one will always look on barrels with a new respect.

Different distillers have different ideas about how their casks are to be treated before they are filled with spirit. Back at Glenfarclas they get their casks from a bodega in Spain, where they have been filled with oloroso sherry for at least three years. All this may seem like an awful lot of trouble just to store whisky, but it is this care for every detail that gives each whisky its own unique quality. Some years ago I visited another Speyside distillery, where I was shown samples of whisky from different types of cask: the spirit stored in plain oak was almost colourless with little aroma; an amontillado cask produced a pale golden spirit with a delicate scent, while the

oloroso was darker and richer. The difference was dramatic.

By law, whisky has to be kept in cask for a minimum of three years, but the longer it is in there, the more it will change in character. The casks are taken off to the bonded warehouses: no duty will yet have been paid. There they join row upon row of other casks, some of which have been there for decades. There the spirit matures, and some simply evaporates – known as 'the angels' share'. At Glenfarclas the minimum time in cask is ten years, but some are even older than that. Whisky is not like wine: it does not go on improving after bottling, so it is only the time in cask that will add to the flavour – and the price. There are even a few bottles of 60-year-old whisky, which sell for thousands of pounds each. Just don't add ginger ale! *CB*

The Pub Sign Artist

It is perfectly possible to enjoy a pint of cider or beer, or a dram of whisky, in the comfort of your own home, but there is for many of us an extra pleasure in taking our favourite tipple in a traditional pub. These days, however, it is not that easy to find what you are looking for in the world of gastro pubs, and pubs punctuated by multiple television screens or playing music that the landlord assumes, usually incorrectly, you might want to hear. One thing that at least offers hope is a genuine hand-painted pub sign, an indication at the very least that someone respects tradition. And if the sign happens to hang outside a pub in the West Country, chances are it was painted by Andrew Grundon in his Signature Signs studio at St Breward in Cornwall.

Andrew had always wanted to be a painter, but of a rather more conventional type. But, as he said, starving in a garret may be romantic in grand opera, but tends to be less so in real life. Then he heard that the St Austell brewery was looking for a sign painter, applied for the job and got it. He soon discovered that the job entailed a good deal more than simply painting attractive pictures. Fortunately, the old sign writer stayed on for a while to teach him the specialist skills, from lettering to applying gold leaf. The latter skill is certainly one you need to master in a hurry: there is no cheap imitation here; this is genuine gold he's working with. Since then, he has become established with his own business, still working for St Austell as well as for many independent pubs. It was only after he had been working for some time that he discovered his grandfather had actually been a sign painter and he inherited, and cherishes, some of his old brushes.

The paintings have to be bold: no one's going to see the detail unless they get up a step ladder, for most signs hang well above head height, and the materials have to stand up to the British climate. Andrew paints with enamel on wood and the result is work that matures rather than simply looking scruffy with age. In many cases he can use his own imagination, but there are times when he has to spend a good deal of time on research. When he did a sign for the North Inn in the heart of Cornwall's old tin- and copper-mining district, for example, he used an underground scene, and he could be absolutely certain that if what he depicted was the least bit

Andrew Grundon in his Cornish studio.

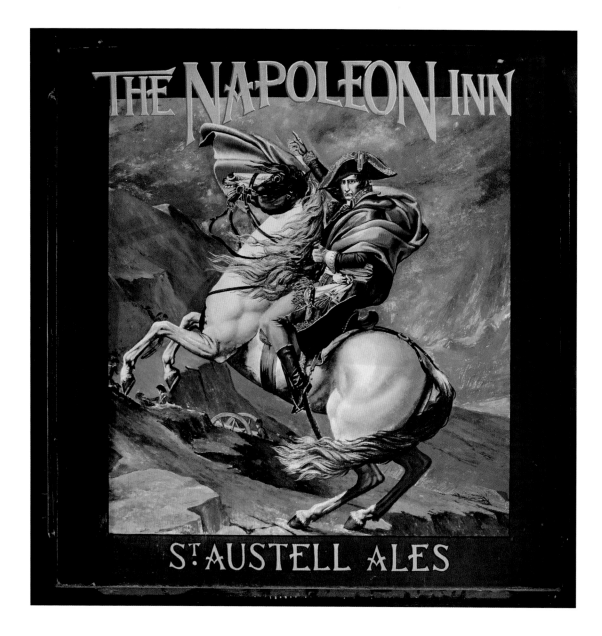

A fine example of Andrew's work based on a famous painting of Napoleon by the French artist Jacques-Louis David.

inaccurate, there'd be a queue of locals at his door telling him where he'd gone wrong. The biggest test comes with any pub where the name involves the Something-or-other Arms. This usually calls for the appropriate heraldic shield, and there is no room for error.

Some pubs present a real challenge. The Bucket of Blood can be found near Hayle in Cornwall. It gets its name from an old story dating back to the 18th century, when a local went to get water from a well near the pub, and when he pulled up the bucket he found it contained a human head. Now the sight of a severed head is not guaranteed to attract customers, so what

Andrew painted was the horrified man at the well, without showing what had astonished him. So it was true to the story – and provided an intriguing mystery for anyone passing by, who, even if they didn't fancy a pint, might pop in to find out what it was all about.

That surely is the great thing about the good pub sign: it is not just an advert for some standard brand, but is individually tailored to each pub to tell its own particular story. The good news is that Andrew is busier than ever, so we can only hope that the traditional pub is thriving in the shadow of its traditional sign.

CB

Above: Andrew at work on a new sign for the London Inn, Padstow.

Left: Applying gold leaf to a St Austell brewery pub sign.

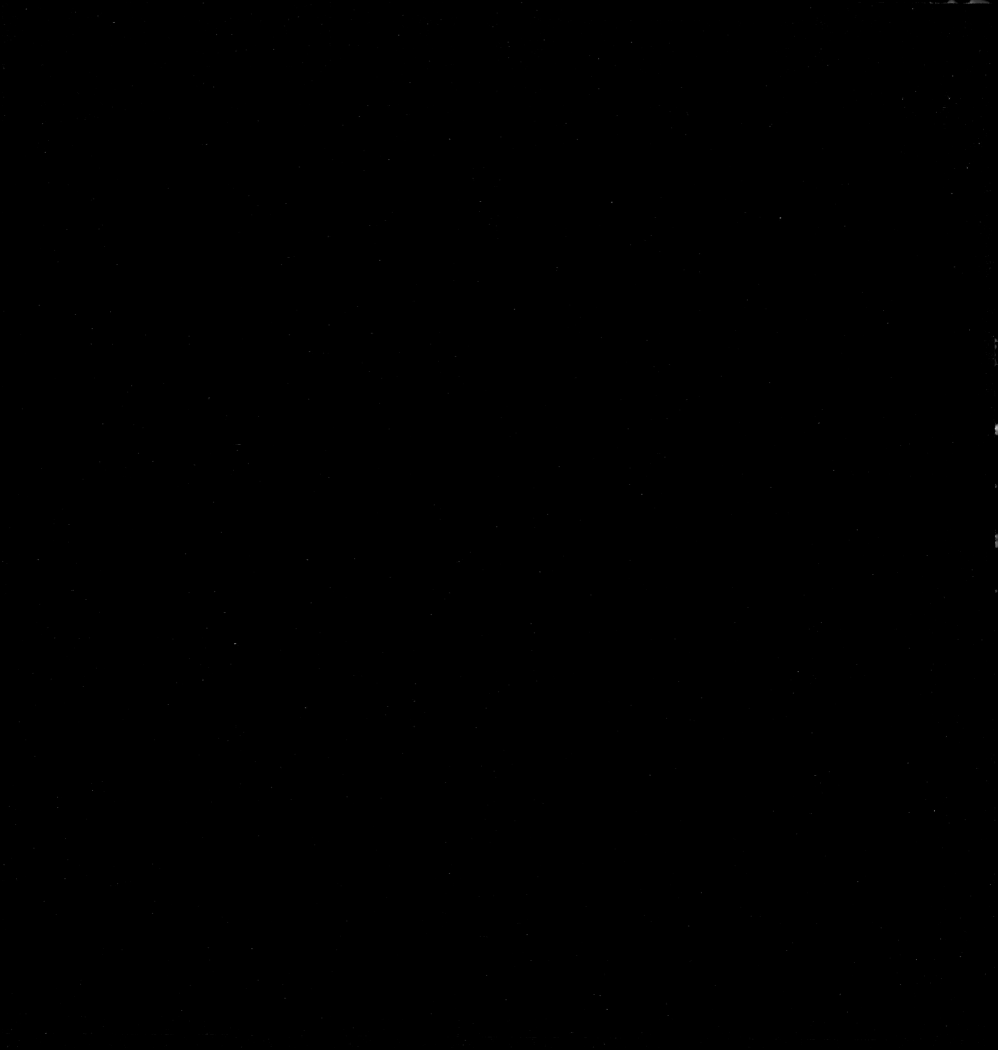

The Church

The
Bell
Foundry

It is not difficult to imagine how the resonant noise of one piece of metal striking another could be used to call a community together, for all kinds of reasons, from attending a religious ceremony to warning of danger from attack. The main thing would be simply to make a noise that was unmistakable and could be heard over a long distance. At some point it was realised that resonance increases if you shape the metal into a sort of bowl shape, which eventually emerged into the familiar bell. For most of us, whatever our religious beliefs, bells are associated with the church, and churches are still some of the most beautiful buildings in our community. It is only appropriate, then, that in calling people to the services or to announce special occasions, the sound of the bells should be as attractive as the churches that house them.

Early European bells were made out of iron plates riveted together and the sound produced was still little better than a metallic clamour. If something more harmonious was required then the technology had to become a great deal more sophisticated. Once a bell had been made that produced a pleasant noise, the same technology could be adapted to make bells tuned to different notes, which could then be used to ring out a melody or, as in English churches, rung in sequences that changed to follow set patterns. The magnificent bells that ring out from parish churches and cathedrals are complex instruments. They do not simply go 'dong': each bell has its own harmonics. Producing such bells is the work of the bell founder.

John Taylor and Co of Loughborough is one of only two bell foundries left in Britain. They have been making bells since 1784 and moved to their present site in 1839 and use methods that have scarcely changed since bells were first cast in the area in the 14th century. The red brick factory, tucked away down a suburban street, has little to distinguish it from hundreds of other old industrial buildings, giving very little hint of what goes on in there, unless you happen to be passing by when the bells in the campanile are playing, or on a casting day, when the roar of the furnace can be clearly heard. Stepping inside feels like walking into the 19th century – and a 19th-century visitor would recognise many of the machines, which is not surprising since that is when some of them arrived new at the foundry. But visitors must not expect to see the whole process in one visit: the bell is a complex instrument and so too is its manufacture.

The outer casing of a bell mould has just been removed from the overhead gantry crane after the bell has been cast.

Top: Bell moulds lined up in the trench dug in the casting house floor at Taylor's bell foundry.

Above: Open boxes being set on top of the moulds to act as reservoirs for the molten metal.

Opposite: Molten bell metal from the furnace being tipped into the moulds. At this stage, the trench has been refilled and the tops of the moulds are at ground level.

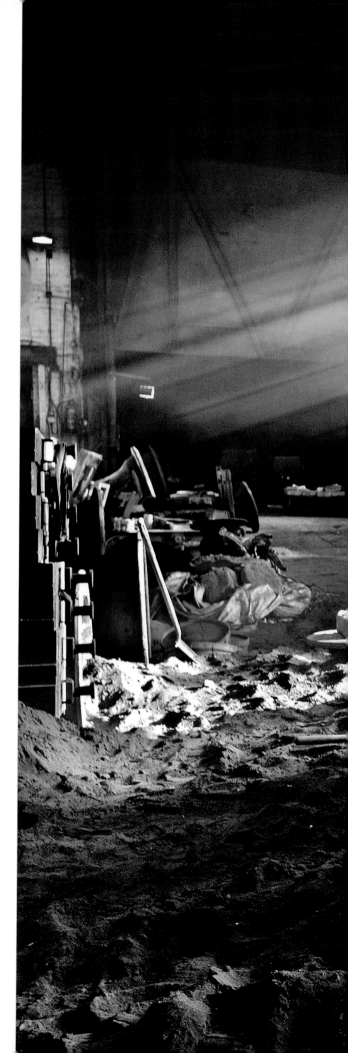

Left: The remains of the mould being cleaned off a bell after casting.

Opposite: At the end of casting, after the metal has cooled, the bell and its casing are lifted from the trench.

The first stage in preparation involves creating a mould for casting the bell, and the elements required are sand, clay, horse manure and straw. They may seem unlikely ingredients, but there is a logic in their use. The fibrous matter in the manure and the straw tend to burn away, leaving minuscule holes through which hot gases can escape without ruining the mould. As generations have proved, this is just the right mixture for a successful result, so why change the recipe? The materials are mixed together and shaped, rather as one might make a giant pot, so that the outer surface will determine the internal profile of the bell. From years of experience, the bell makers know just what shape is needed for each particular bell, and a wooden former is used to smooth the whole thing off, to create the core. The outer part of the mould, the case, is then prepared and lowered over the core. The two parts are then clamped into place, leaving a space in between into which the molten metal will be poured. Normally several moulds would be prepared at the same time for casting a number of bells.

The foundry has a floor of black sand. On casting day, the furnace is fired up to melt the bell metal, a form of bronze, normally 78 per cent copper and 22 per cent tin. The ratio is crucial to ensure just the right combination of resonance and resilience to fracturing. As the metal is brought up to temperature, the rest of the preparations continue. A trench is dug in the black sand of the foundry floor and the moulds are lowered into it, so that the top of each mould is at ground level. When everything is in place, the sand is shovelled back in and packed tightly leaving just the tops of the moulds on the surface. Open-topped boxes are attached to the tops to take the molten metal, so that when it is poured no air is trapped. When everything is ready, the whole furnace is tilted and the molten metal poured into a giant ladle. Slag is scooped off the surface, the metal is degassed and then the ladle is moved to each of the castings, where the metal is carefully poured and released into the moulds. At this point everything has to stop for three or four days to let the metal cool down, the close-packed sand ensuring that this is a slow, even process. After that the mould is broken open and the new bells revealed. But we are still very far from the end of the process.

A new bell may look magnificent as it emerges from its mould, like a butterfly from a chrysalis, but it now has to be tuned. It is taken to the tuning shop, where a big bell will be placed on a vertical lathe with a rotating turntable, a magnificent machine that has remained in use for well over a century. There are the more familiar horizontal lathes for use with smaller bells. Taylor's introduced their five principal harmonics method of tuning in 1896, and they have never needed to change it in any fundamental way. The bell is struck at different points to be assessed by the Bell Master.

The casing is lifted from the newly cast bell, with traces
of the mould still clinging to the shiny metal.

Left: The vertical lathe is used to delicately shave off slivers of metal to bring the bell perfectly into tune.

Originally, he would have used tuning forks, and there is a splendid array of them in the shop's office, ranging from the sort that you might expect to be used by a soprano looking for the starting note to monstrous pieces of iron that could poleaxe a bull. But this is the one area of the works where modern technology has taken over – now all you need is a microphone and a suitably programmed laptop. However, once the Bell Master has decided what needs doing it still requires a great deal of skill from the Bell Tuner to follow his instructions. The tuner has to cut away the inside of the bell by carefully controlling the lathe and an error here could turn a beautiful bell into scrap – you can take metal away but you can never stick it back on.

When the Bell Master is happy, the bell will be given the final trial – it's taken to the test rig and rung. Only then can it be sent away to the client, and clients come from around the world. When we visited, there were bells being cast for Truro Cathedral and one bell for a temple in Sri Lanka. The process of casting and tuning a bell may be slow and may look antiquated, but it is the final result that matters and no one has yet found a better way of doing it.

In British churches it is normal for bells to be swung round in a full circle, and they have to be set in a special frame. Taylor's also make the frame, and they would also expect to carry out the final process of setting the bell in its own tower.

CB

Top: Before electronic tuning became available, tuning forks had to be used – the larger forks sound the deeper tones.

Above: The Taylor foundry with the campanile on the corner.

The Stained Glass Studio

Today, we tend to think of stained glass windows – or at any rate the best of them – as works of art, but originally they were set in place not as decoration but to reinforce a message. In an age when most of the population was illiterate, they told stories. Some of the most dramatic examples can be seen in the church at Fairford in Gloucestershire. There are 28 medieval windows in all, and the most striking represent Heaven and Hell. They are intended to remind the congregation of the glories they can expect if they lead good Christian lives; and conversely, just what horrors lie in wait for the wicked. The grinning demons are literally meant to put the fear of God into you. They survive today because of a long process of careful restoration that began in 1987 and was only completed in 2010. It was the work of the Barley Studio on York.

As a boy, Keith Barley was always being taken to look at churches, whether by his mother, who had a keen interest in church history, or by his grandmother, who was fascinated by gravestones. Few buildings in Britain can boast finer stained glass than York Minster, and it was there he went as an apprentice at the York Glaziers Trust to learn his trade. As he explained, you cannot be a conservator unless you fully understand the materials you work with – what they can and cannot do. Before you can be a stained glass restorer, you must first learn the craft.

Since he set up his own studio in 1973, he has worked on many major projects and has never lost his passion for conservation. During our visit, he was working on nine 16th-century windows from Lichfield Cathedral. They were removed with extreme care, replaced by plain glass as a temporary measure, and brought to the studio. Seeing the fragments laid out was like viewing a nightmare jigsaw that it seemed impossible to ever put back together again. That is where the craft of the restorer comes in. He was also putting the finishing touches to a window for a 19th-century museum and gallery, the Beaney House of Art and Knowledge in Canterbury.

It was while working on the Fairford windows that he took an important decision. Much medieval glass had been lost during the Reformation, when Puritans destroyed the 'Papist' images, but Fairford was different: the windows here were damaged during the great storm of 1703, and later restoration had muddled things up. The general rule of conservation

Keith Barley at work restoring a stained glass window for
the Beaney House of Art and Knowledge in Canterbury.

Helen Whittaker preparing paint for a new window that
will be installed in Westminster Abbey.

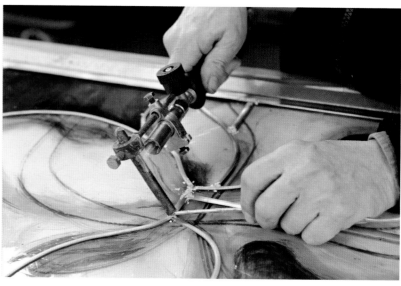

An essential element in a stained glass window is the leading,
which secures the glass pieces and delineates outlines.

at that time was to treat a window as simply something to be preserved as it was at the time they started to work on it, with no additions or attempts at replacement of missing parts. But Keith believed it was more important to restore the windows so that they reflected the original artist's intention, and told the story he was trying to tell. Where necessary, he would insert and paint a new piece to create the image. It had also become common to use much heavier leading than would have been used by medieval glaziers. Sometimes, it could be as much as 3/8 of an inch thick; Keith, however, would normally use between 1/8 and 3/16, making the image far clearer and closer to its original appearance.

Once completed, the new window would be protected by a system of iso-thermic plating. The new stained glass is hung, rather like a picture, in front of a new plain glass window. The plain glass provides protection against the weather and any objects that might cause damage, from a bird to a pebble from a lawnmower. Equally importantly, because the space between the two layers is at the same temperature as the body of the building, the glass will not be affected by condensation. Throughout the process of conservation and replacement, Keith keeps a careful record of exactly what was done so that if attitudes change at some date in the future, changes can be reversed.

The studio also creates new windows as well as restoring the old. Keith is a firm believer in the apprenticeship system as the best way of learning his craft. One of those apprentices was Helen Whittaker. When she was a student at art school, her tutor remarked on the fact that she liked adding

heavy outlines to her work to emphasise the subject matter. The lines reminded him of the leading in windows and he suggested she might like to try designing stained glass. She came to the Barley Studio and Keith was so impressed that he kept a place open for her while she completed her MA. Now she is back and designing full time.

The process starts with carefully measuring the window space to be filled and making a paper template. The next stage is to produce a coloured design for the client, and when that has been approved, the actual work can begin. The original design is used as the basis for a 'cartoon' – not a comic strip, but a full-sized pencil drawing. Using a tracing of the cartoon, the lead lines are marked in, indicating where the leading that holds the glass will be placed. From this tracing, the coloured glasses can be cut to the correct shape and laid out on the cartoon. The finished window will not just be an assemblage of coloured glasses: it will be painted over to create a more intricate and interesting design. The paint is actually mixed with powdered glass and when the work is complete it is heated in a kiln. The powdered glass, when heated, bonds the paint firmly to the glass background.

The work is completed by leading. The lead does more than simply hold the glass pieces in place: it can also be used to help create the pattern – just as Helen's heavy pencil strokes did in her art school drawings. Now the whole window is ready for installation. On my first visit to York, Helen was working on designs for Westminster Abbey. The work is now complete and installed in all its glory. *CB*

Helen painting panels that are held up against the natural light so that she can be sure she is creating the right effect.

Above and left: Completed panels laid out in the kiln ready for firing to fix the colours.

Opposite: The east window in Dunnington Church, made and designed by the Barley Studio.

The completed windows in place in the Lady Chapel at
Westminster Abbey: the central section was designed
and made by the late Alan Younger.

The Organ Builder

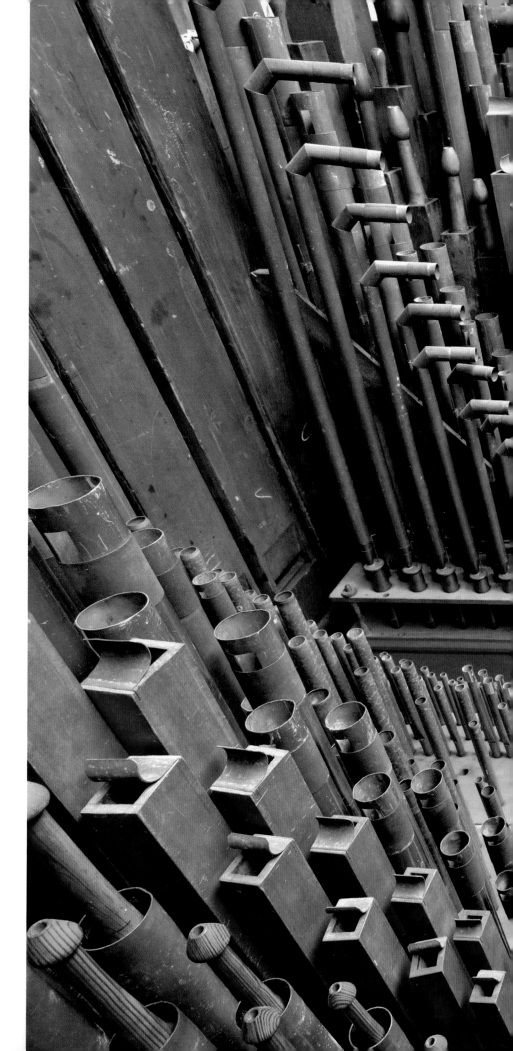

Henry Willis & Sons have been building organs since the company was founded by 'Father' Henry Willis in 1845. Since then they have built over 2,500 pipe organs that have been installed in churches and halls around the world, as well as restoring thousands more. Before describing the work that goes on in their workshops in Liverpool, it is as well to get at least an idea of what goes into making an organ. We went across the Mersey to Port Sunlight, where the church has one of the best preserved of all the Willis church organs, built by Henry Willis II and installed in 1904. Now I am probably like most people in having a vague idea of how an organ works. Air is blown into pipes to create the different notes, and stops are used to alter the way in which the notes sound. We look at a fine church organ such as this, with its handsome array of pipes, and assume that is more or less it. But if you think more carefully, and look at the console, you find there are three keyboards as well as the foot pedals and an imposing array of knobs for the different stops. There has to be more to it than can be seen from the outside.

I was taken by Jonathan Bowden, who is both a director of the company and the church organist, into the vestry and through a door into the organ case. There is a veritable jungle of pipes of all shapes and sizes, hugely impressive but not quite as grand as the biggest of all the Willis organs. Built in the 1920s for Liverpool Cathedral, it had an astonishing 10,268 pipes. That was only part of the Port Sunlight story. Back in the vestry again, he lifted a trap door and we went down to the cellar beneath the organ, where the giant bellows are housed, fed by an electric blower with five fans in series. Originally, the bellows were powered by water – the river was diverted under the church when the organ was being played full throttle. If only one of the keyboards and a few stops were needed, it could be fed by hand. This business of building an organ was far more complicated than I had ever imagined. Managing director David Wyld made the point that until the Industrial Revolution of the late 18th century, the pipe organ was the most complex mechanism ever made by man.

In many respects the organ works look much like any other light engineering works, with machines for working both wood and metal. It is the way

Assembling the pipework for an organ at Henry Willis & Sons: a rare glimpse of the complexity that lies behind the façade of a church organ.

116

Preparing an air chest with its valves that
direct the air to the appropriate organ pipes.

Pipes are being tuned by adjusting their pitch to notes played on
the keyboard.

they work that distinguishes them from other apparently similar firms. This
is a community of craft workers and they are working much as organ builders
have done for centuries. Here, they are following the written rules that were
laid down when the company was new over a century and a half ago.

The starting point is the organ pipe. How they are built depends on
their size. Organ builders generally rely on specialised suppliers, though
roughly 20 per cent are made here. The smaller pipes are made out of a soft
alloy, mainly consisting of lead, with added tin as a stiffener together with
smaller quantities of other elements such as bismuth and antimony. The
pipe metal can be made on the premises, the mixture of metals heated and
then poured in a molten state into a trough, where it is smoothed out into
even sheets. Beyond a certain size, however, the metal proves too soft and
buckles. The larger pipes are generally made out of zinc, though wood can
also be used. Some organs have smaller wooden pipes as well, but because
of their intricacy, these are made by outside joiners.

Organ pipes come in two basic varieties – plain tubes, known as 'flues',
and reed pipes, containing a vibrating tongue. The tongues act just like
the reeds in wind instruments and are used to produce similar effects, so
you'll find on the console that there are knobs labelled with familiar names,
such as clarinet and oboe. The tongues themselves are made of brass and
have to be accurately curved. For smaller pipes this can be done by hand,
but for the larger versions they use a unique machine invented by the company in the 19th century. This uses an elaborate array of springs and levers,

operated by wheels and handles. Assembling the pipes involves far more
than simply putting together the various bits and pieces. Pipes have to be
fine-tuned to provide an accurate note. The keyboards for Wallis organs
generally have a compass of 61 notes, from bottom C to top C, covering all
the naturals, sharps and flats. That is only a part of the story. In the voicing
room, pipes are sounded together a semitone apart to produce the correct
timbre. There is only one test applied: the acute ear of the tuner, who makes
the necessary fine adjustments.

It is all very well having an array of pipes, each accurately tuned and
sounding perfectly together, but there has to be a mechanism to get air
into the correct pipe to make the right sound. Except that, in the world
of organ builders, it isn't called air – it's wind. The essential idea is simple enough. Bellows provide the air that is fed into a reservoir at above
normal atmospheric pressure. When the organist depresses a key or a
pedal, he is directing the wind to a pipe of that value, say middle C. He
can also pull out a stop, which will dictate whether the wind goes to an
open flue or to one of the many varieties of reed pipe. The mechanism for
doing this is simple in theory: he is activating a valve that, in effect, acts to
switch a particular pipe on or off. In practice, it is inevitably far more complex.

At the base of the system is the sounding board with holes in the
upper surface. Above that is the chest, which slides above it. Each chest has
holes to take a particular group of pipes. It is here that the whole movement is controlled through movable valves and membranes. Chests have

Selecting a metal organ pipe
from the store.

Fine-tuning adjustment being made by
slightly opening up the top of a pipe.

A magnificent example of a Willis organ in Christ Church, Port Sunlight.

to be made with as much care as the pipes, with each element made with great accuracy – yet another skilled job – involving working with materials of wood, metal and leather. There are three ways of moving the different parts to open and close off the flow of wind to a particular pipe: purely mechanical, hydraulic and electric. Whichever is used, the actual system is the same as it always has been. As David Wyld said, nothing has really changed, everything is done just as it always was, not because they are old-fashioned, but simply because no one has ever found a better way.

When assembled, the keyboards and pedals are used with different groups of pipes: in a comparatively modest organ, with just two keyboards, one will relate to one set, and the other to a different set, and the pedals will be confined to the lower registers. By combining all these sounds, the organ is capable of an immense variety of tones and colours. There is nothing else quite like it: certainly not the modern electronic versions. David Wyld's view of the modern intruders was succinct: 'All right to practise on.' The pipe organ remains unique. Perhaps the last words should be those inscribed in Latin on the original plaque on the Port Sunlight organ: they can be translated as 'through the ears to the soul'. *CB*

Building Materials

The Stone Quarry

Historically, builders have used the materials that were most readily available in the area where they were working. In the more distant past, many buildings were timber-framed, the spaces filled with wattle and daub, but for the past few centuries the main choice has been between stone and brick. If good-quality freestone was easily accessed then that would be used, and one can see great variations throughout the country, from the mellow limestone of the Cotswolds to the darkened gritstone of the Pennines. Elsewhere, clay was dug and fired locally to make bricks. But even in regions where brick was the norm, stone was still valued and used for the grandest and most important buildings – and was considered more or less essential for churches.

Different stones have different characteristics, but some were especially treasured, and among these was the oolitic limestone from quarries on the Isle of Purbeck. The most highly prized form of the limestone was laid down in the Jurassic period when the region was underwater, covered by rivers and shallow lagoons. Countless small shellfish were crushed together to form the stone, and in the case of the marble it is given its very special character because the shells are predominantly of a little freshwater snail. The shells have crystallised to form a very hard stone that can be polished, and this brings out the typical marbling pattern. It has been valued for many centuries: archives in the Tower of London record the Archbishop of Canterbury ordering stone from Purbeck for Chichester Cathedral in 1205, and examples can be found right back to Roman times. Although marble has made Purbeck famous, it is only one type of limestone quarried at Purbeck and the other varieties have also proved their value over the years for everything from paving to memorials. It is still quarried today, and we visited the Haysom quarry at St Aldhelm's Head near Worth Matravers.

We arrived, after bouncing down a rough track, at the quarry with its somewhat ramshackle collection of buildings, put together with whatever was at hand – breeze blocks, corrugated iron, but not much stone. These are buildings that are strictly functional, with not the least pretension to any architectural quality whatsoever. An obvious question is – why is the quarry so deep? Looking at the exposed rock face, stone starts just below the surface of the soil. The answer is that the rock at the very top is completely useless, and the layers beneath that have different characteristics.

Turning Purbeck marble on a lathe at the Haysom quarry.

A general view of the quarry at St Aldhelm's Head, Dorset.

The quarry
office interior.

The hard limestone favoured by letter carvers is right at the bottom.

In the past, explosives were used: generally in this quarry just simple black powder. It must have been an interesting time: Brian, who was among the last to use the method at this quarry, remembers one firing when one huge rock sailed right out of the quarry to land in a field. Today, one big machine simply grabs the rock out of the quarry face. These great pieces of rock are often too big to handle so need to be split, and the technique used is one that has been practised for centuries. A straight line is drawn across the block where the split is to be made. A series of holes are then drilled into the stone. Wedges are inserted and hammered down.

The first stage in creating stone slabs is to split a huge block by feathering: holes are drilled and wedges inserted.

The wedges are hammered down until
the rock splits.

One of the split sections is then taken into the workshop and placed on the
bed of a multi-bladed mechanical saw to be cut into thin slabs.

Nothing much seems to happen at first, though the sound of the hammer
blow subtly changes. Then, quite suddenly, the crack widens and the two
sections can be levered apart: one rock has become two.

The first stage is often rough dressing, removing unwanted material
from the block by hand. As with the splitting, nothing has changed much
over the years: it is still a case of hitting metal punches with a hammer. The
punches need to be kept sharp, which would once have meant regular visits
to the local blacksmith, but there are few local blacksmiths to be found
these days, so the quarry has its own forge. This must be one of the smallest
forges anywhere and, like the other buildings on site, has been put together
out of oddments, including a window with about half the panes either
broken or missing altogether. It is just a hearth for heating the metal and a
bucket of water for quenching. Some stones are roughly dressed by hand as
well: during the visit we saw two men busily preparing blocks for farm walls.

The quarry produces no standard items – everything is done to the customers' orders – and many of the orders are for slabs, either for paving or for memorial stones. The process begins by bringing one of the big cut blocks into
the main shed on a forklift truck, then fastening slings to lift it by overhead
crane onto the bed of a giant circular saw. The block is levelled up by the simple
process of using a crowbar as a lever and placing a wedge under the end that
needs to be raised. Then the powered, water-cooled spray goes into action in
a cloud of droplets and dust, carving into the stone to create a straight edge.

To split the block into slabs it is next moved to the band saw. This is
a machine that, apart from the electric motor, could probably have been
seen in the 19th century or even earlier. The motor is used to drive a large
flywheel, with a crank that converts the circular motion of the wheel to the
to-and-fro action of the saw. There are 13 blades, so the saw can produce up
to 12 slabs from any one block. A preset screw moves the blades downwards
through the block at a stately 9 inches an hour. Once the blocks are cut, they
need to be smoothed to remove the saw marks and any imperfections. They
are laid on a bench covered with what was once someone's carpet and a car-
borundum polisher is passed over them. If necessary, they can be given a final
polish by hand. Some stone takes a much higher degree of polishing. A beautiful slab of what looked as if it might be the famous Purbeck marble, but was
actually known much more prosaically as Purbeck Grub, was being prepared
as a tabletop for a famous location – Lord's cricket ground.

Not all stone is turned into slabs. A quite exotic order had been received
from Italy for stone that was to form part of a mosaic floor, copying one in
Westminster Abbey and for classical pillars. The pillars have to be turned
on a lathe, a process identical to the familiar one of wood turning, apart
from the fact that the material to be worked is a good deal harder. There
was a time when far more elaborate carvings were produced here for large
churches and cathedrals, but nowadays the stone is only roughed out at the
quarry and is sent on for finishing. *CB*

The full beauty of Purbeck marble is revealed after the stone
has been turned and polished.

The Stonemasons

There is probably no finer place to see craftsmanship in stone than in one of the great cathedrals, and few are grander or more ornate than Salisbury. The foundation stone was laid in 1220 and the famous spire was added a century later. It was built of the finest stone available, but even the best suffers over time, and the cathedral's team of masons are embarked on a major renovation programme. The area currently being worked on is high up on the outside of the building and the only way to see what is being done and why is to climb the ladders up the scaffolding. Just below the roof is a blind arcade, in effect a parapet consisting of a series of arches – blind because the space inside the arch is also stone, instead of either glass or an opening. Corners are marked by more ornate pinnacles. What is remarkable is the way in which the masons have produced a structure of great beauty, with each arch elaborately carved, even though few visitors will ever get to see it, nor even be aware of the complexity of the work if they do look up.

Mason Alan Spittle was taking careful measurements of badly worn areas, using callipers and a tape measure, which together with tracings would be used to produce accurate drawings from which a template would then be made for a replacement. Later the old piece would be cut out and the new inserted, and it is essential that everything is accurately matched: the modern workmanship has to be of the same high standard as that of the medieval masons who first came here eight centuries ago.

Back at ground level, in the workshops another mason, Jamie Woolrich Moon, was at work carving part of a mullion, the vertical section of one of the arches. Stone had already been cut into a squared-off block, using a saw very similar to that in use at the quarry. Jamie's job was to create the complex rounded surfaces of the outside face. The technology has not changed for hundreds of years. He works as his predecessors did, with mallet and chisel, slowly and carefully removing the stone, first in straight lines, then, as the shape gets nearer to that of the required curve, beginning the task of chamfering. Up on the scaffolding it was easy to see just how well he and the other masons have done their work, the old and new fitting together in perfect harmony.

At times more elaborate work is needed: Alan had earlier been asked to carve an angel's head, which sadly is now difficult to see, having been rather ignominiously hidden behind new toilets. With this kind of work, the first stage is to model the figure in clay, and then produce a plaster cast from the model. Once this has been approved by the architect, the plaster cast will be used as the maquette for the finished carving. Alan's work may be temporarily lost from sight, but he has the satisfaction of knowing it will still be there long after the intruding loos have gone. And this is true of all the renovation work that will be continuing for many years to come: the masons are working not for the short-term effect, but for posterity.

CB

From far left: Work on renewing the fabric of Salisbury Cathedral is an ongoing process. It begins by taking accurate measurements of parts that need replacing due to wear and tear – in this case a marble column high on the roof and a stone cross. The extensive scaffolding gives an idea of the scale of the operation.

Right: A craftsman in the workshop, shaping a block that will eventually have smooth curves to fit the marked outline.

The
Brickworks

Man has been making bricks for more than 10,000 years, and the technology changed little over the centuries, until comparatively recent times. Look at a modern housing development and you will almost certainly find that it uses bricks that are all exactly the same size, colour and texture. It was not always so. By contrast, if you look at any brick building from the 18th century or earlier, things seem very different: here you will find subtle gradations of colour and texture that give walls a richness that is lacking in much of what we can see all around us today.

We have a wealth of old brick buildings in this country, but like all structures they need restoration and repair from time to time, and that creates a problem. Add modern bricks to the old and the result is like sticking a patch of garish synthetic material onto an ancient tapestry. The restorers who are sensitive to preserving the old need to turn to someone who is making bricks using an older technology than the wholly mechanised systems at use in modern brickyards. They are most likely to end up knocking at the door of Bulmer Brick and Tile Works in Suffolk. They have been making bricks in this area using London clay since the Middle Ages, and Bulmer continue the tradition.

The story starts at the clay pit where the raw material is extracted. The first stage in the processing is to put the clay through a pug mill, which is simply a machine that thoroughly mixes the clay to get a uniform material and removes any air bubbles that could cause the brick to burst in the kiln. The bricks themselves are still individually made by hand. The brick maker takes a quantity of clay and throws it into a mould. This is simply a wooden box, but without top or bottom. The dimensions are very traditional: the length of the brick is twice the width and the width is twice the height: 4-2-1. The clay is firmly packed and any excess scraped off for reuse. The brick is then placed onto a barrow and the mould pulled away. Once a barrow is full it is wheeled away to the open-sided drying sheds, known as 'hacks', where the bricks are stacked in long rows to gradually dry out until they are ready to go to the kiln for firing. It all looks very straightforward, but for a beginner trying his hand at brick making, it is nowhere near as easy as it looks. It seems to take a long time

Unloading the kiln at Bulmer Brick and Tile Works after the hand-made bricks have been fired.

Stoking the fire in the brick kiln.

The beehive or updraft kiln: the openings in the roof are closed off during firing and opened up again afterwards to allow the kiln to cool down.

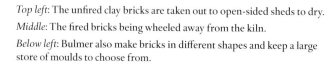

Top left: The unfired clay bricks are taken out to open-sided sheds to dry.

Middle: The fired bricks being wheeled away from the kiln.

Below left: Bulmer also make bricks in different shapes and keep a large store of moulds to choose from.

Opposite: Making a brick by hand by pressing clay into the mould.

to get the perfect oblong brick, but the experienced brick maker can make around 900 bricks by hand in the working day.

The really important difference between this brickyard and its modern counterpart is the kiln itself. This is a wonderful building that demonstrates just what a difference it makes using the old technologies, with a pantile roof of amazingly varied colours. This is a type known as both a beehive kiln and a downdraught kiln: the former name gives an idea of what it looks like, the latter how it works. Kilns like this were first used in China during the Ming dynasty but didn't appear in Europe until the 19th century. The Bulmer kiln is circular with stoking holes all round the outside. The dried bricks are stacked inside – a long job taking two days as the kiln holds 12,000 bricks. The distinguishing feature is the tall chimney at the edge of the main kiln. As the fire heats up, the hot gases rise over the bricks and are then sucked back down through the brick stack to leave by way of the chimney via holes in the floor. The fires reach a temperature of 1100°C and it requires a great deal of skill to keep everything at an even temperature. Any change in the strength of the wind can have an effect, so the rate at which the gases leave the chimney has to be regulated. The process of firing the bricks – known here as tanning – takes 36 hours. Then there has to be a period of another two days for everything to cool down before the bricks can be removed, another two-day job. One can see why modern brickworks all use a continuous system – but one can

The temperature of the kiln has to be regularly checked during firing.

also see how the finished product at Bulmer is very different. The colours vary from a deep red to a rich purple. No colour is added: the variations all occur naturally in the firing.

Bulmer do not just make oblong bricks. They also produce 'rubbed' bricks to order. These are basically bricks that are produced not in the standard oblongs but in a variety of different shapes. There is a special workshop where, instead of being moulded to shape, the brick is shaped using a wire cutter worked against a wooden pattern. There is a staggering variety of 'standard' shapes available, about 5,000 of them in different sizes. And if what you want isn't available off the shelf,

then they can make shapes to your specific requirements, working from architects' drawings. This service is invaluable in the world of building restoration, and Bulmer have supplied brick for some highly prestigious projects, from chimneys for Hampton Court to the arches for the recently refurbished St Pancras station.

Without family run businesses such as Bulmer it is difficult to see how building restoration could proceed with any degree of authenticity. But bricks are not the only building material where modern technology has produced a perfectly good product, well adapted to modern life, but which often sits uneasily in older buildings.

CB

Above: Bricks can be made in many different shades, each of which has its own name.

Right: A magnificent example of Bulmer multi-coloured bricks used in the renovation of St Pancras Station.

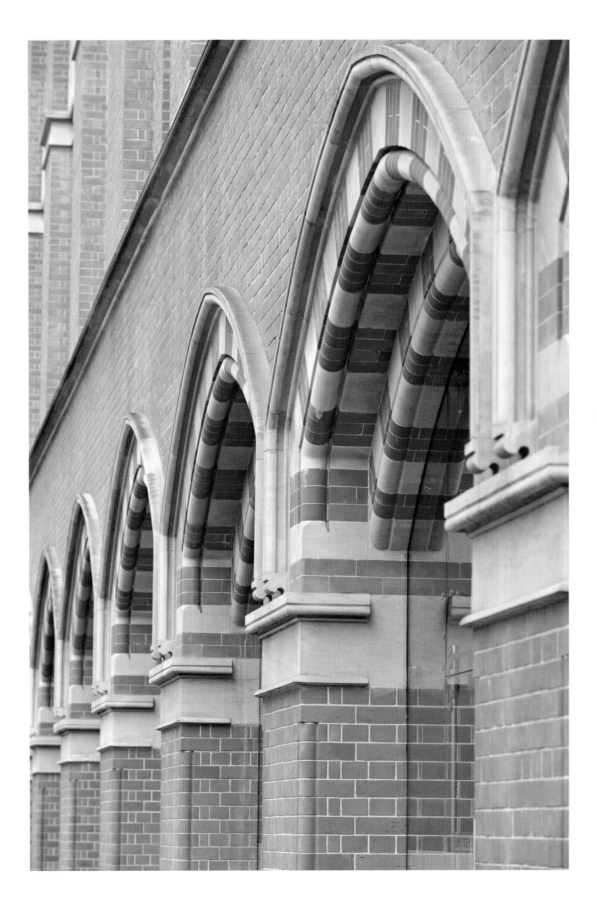

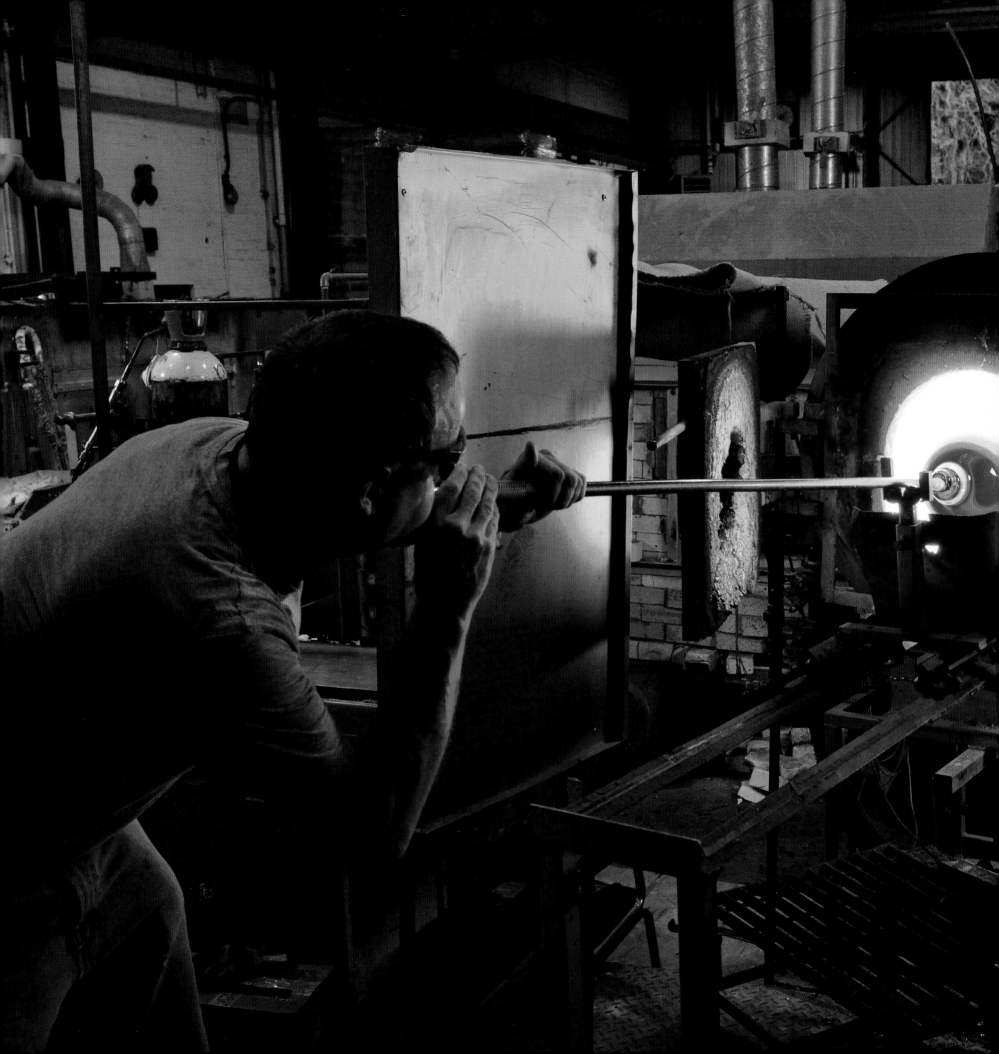

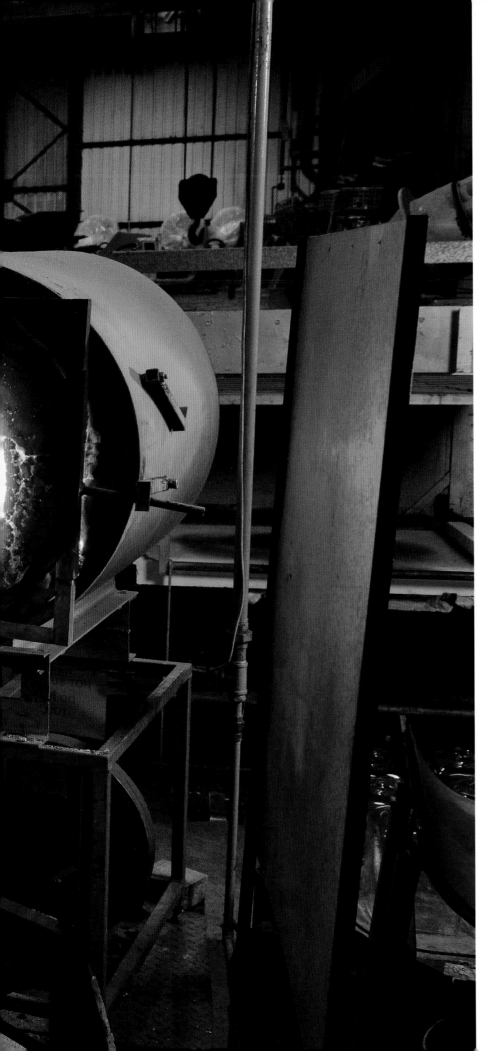

The
Glass Maker

Just as bricks in older buildings look very different from those in more modern constructions, so too window glass has changed over the years. We are used to seeing perfectly transparent, smooth panes, but this was not always the case. Older windows all show slight irregularities – the difference isn't huge but it is quite enough for those who want to do a perfect restoration job to try to replicate the effect, and the best way to do that is to use the technology of the past. Probably most people when they think of 'antique' window glass think of the so-called bulls-eye windows that are often added to new buildings to give some sort of distinction and a feeling of reproducing the best of the past. This is rather odd, because that sort of glass is only a by-product of the glass-making process and would have been sold off cheap for use in the very poorest homes. To understand why, you have to understand the technique used in its manufacture.

The aim of the process was to produce crown glass. It started with an expert glass blower collecting a blob of molten glass on the end of his blowpipe. The aim was to produce a large hollow sphere. Once the maximum size had been reached it was rapidly rotated until centrifugal force had flattened the sphere out into a disc. Panes could then be cut from the edge of the disc and used for windows. It was the central lump that was the bull's eye and as likely to be used in a cowshed as in a house. This was the technique that had been used for centuries, but by the late 18th century an improved method had been introduced for making plate glass.

The new technique began much as the old, with blowing a huge glass bubble, but instead of rotating it into a disc, it was now swung like a pendulum, dragging the sphere out into an elongated sausage shape. This was formed into a cylinder, slit and flattened out. The technology was perfected by Chance Brothers of Birmingham in the 19th century, with the help of a French glassmaker. The great advantage of the method was that far bigger panes could be made than with the older crown glass method – just exactly what was needed when Joseph Paxton came up with his revolutionary design for the Great Exhibition of 1851, the Crystal Palace. Official records show that the building contained an astonishing 293,655 panes of glass – and Chance Brothers were turning them out at a rate of over 60,000 a week. Both techniques are still in use at English Antique Glass at

Blowing glass in one of the furnaces at English Antique Glass.

147

On first leaving the furnace the glass has to be blown
into a perfect globe.

Collecting a blob of molten glass from the furnace, preparatory to the
first blowing.

The glass is gradually shaped by being blown using different moulds.

Swinging the globe of glass gradually elongates it into a cylindrical shape.

The final shaping of the cylinder takes place in another mould.

Alvechurch in Worcestershire, a county that has traditionally been at the heart of English glass manufacture.

The buildings are modern with no hint that inside you'll find a craft being practised that is centuries old. The raw constituents of glass are silica, in the form of fine sand, together with soda and lime. Two furnaces roar away in the works, in the first of which the ingredients fuse together to form molten glass. Whichever type is being made, the process starts in the same way. Here you see craftsmanship of the highest order. The assistant starts by collecting just the right-sized blob of glass on the end of a long, hollow iron rod. He blows it to start a bubble forming and then passes it on to the master craftsman, who now continues the blowing process, increasing the size of the bubble. To ensure it turns into a perfect sphere, the hot glass is regularly reheated and accurately shaped by turning it round and round in increasingly large curved wooden moulds, dampened down with water to prevent them catching fire.

A hole is cut in one end of the cylinder as the blowing process is completed.

The blown cylinder has both ends cut off and a slit is cut down the side – it can then be reheated and flattened out to create pane of glass.

The storeroom with samples of coloured glass panes.

It is then passed on to the second, smaller furnace for further reworking until it has reached exactly the right consistency and size.

The next fascinating part, when plate cylinder glass is being made, comes with the transformation of the glass bubble. It looks impossible that this globule of hot glass can be swung at the end without breaking, but it soon elongates into just the right shape. It now goes back to the assistant who pierces the end of the cylinder with a blowlamp and opens out the end with callipers. The glass is cut from the pipe and shaped to be perfectly symmetrical. It then joins other cylinders in an oven, where the temperature can be controlled and gradually allowed to cool.

The final stage involves cutting a slit in the cylinder, and once there are enough prepared cylinders they set off on their final journey through a tunnel-like device, the lehr. This is a slow passage through the lehr from a cool to a hot end, and by the time it emerges, the cylinder has softened and begun to collapse. It passes onto a bench, where it is smoothed flat with a wooden block and then sent back in the opposite direction, moving from hot back to cool.

You can now see why this glass is special, with minute air bubbles and slight variations in the surface texture. English Antique Glass do not only produce plain glass: there is a regular output of coloured glasses, made by adding chemicals to the basic glass mix. For example, by mixing in manganese and iron oxides, the glass that emerges has a rich amber colour. It is this specialist coloured glass that is invaluable for those working with traditional stained glass windows.

Not all the glass made here goes for windows, plain or stained: there is a steady production of glass for all kinds of other items, from paperweights to vases. But however it is used, the glass made here has a special quality that can never be exactly reproduced by any other technique, and that is why the craft survives. No one has found a better way of meeting so many different, but highly specialised, needs.

CB

151

Working Metal

The
Blacksmith

Traditionally, there have been two basic ways of working with metal that dominated the industry for centuries: the forge where metal was beaten into shape and the foundry, where objects were cast from patterns. Until the 18th century, the former was by far the most important, and there was a time when every community had its forge.

Here two distinct crafts were practised: that of the farrier, who shod horses, and that of the smith, who made all kinds of things out of metal, from fire irons to ornate gates for the local manor house. It was, however, quite normal for one man to fulfil both roles. The arrival of motor vehicles more or less brought an end to the age of the working horse, and today's farriers tend to work with portable outfits that they take to the horses, rather than work from a forge and wait for the horses to come to them. The blacksmith, however, still works much as his ancestors did for generations.

Moretonhampstead was once one of the most important towns on Dartmoor, with its market and annual fair. Its importance declined when the local wool trade petered out but it remains a busy tourist centre. Horses no longer queue up to be shod at the Moreton Forge, but it remains as busy as it has been at any time in the 150 years or so it has been there. It is not a difficult place to find: the sign on Cross Street shows a blacksmith at work. It is more than just an indication of where the forge can be found; it is itself a celebration of the skill of the current blacksmith, Greg Abel. The actual forge is next to the yard behind the house.

Going into the forge is to enter what at first sight seems an incomprehensible jumble of things, with just a few recognisable points of reference. There are the hearth and the anvil and a variety of tools all over the place,

Above: Greg Abel made his own sign to hang outside his forge in Moretonhampstead.

155

Removing scale from white hot metal during forging.

but there are also machines that would not have been present a century ago. Greg has modernised, though not exactly adding the latest in technology. The most prominent item is a Blacker forge hammer, which is certainly well over half a century old. I found an advert, dating from 1942, put out by the company based in Stalybridge in Lancashire, claiming that there were 'over 4,000 in use'. The machine was actually patented some 20 years earlier. There certainly aren't that many now and although I've visited many industrial sites over the years, this was the first I'd ever seen. Basically, it's a direct descendant of the old tilt hammers, except that power comes from an electric motor instead of a waterwheel. The motor turns an eccentric cam that engages with the shaft of the hammer, raising the head and then, as the cam moves round, allowing the hammerhead to drop back onto the metal placed on the anvil. It does the same job as the blacksmith wielding a hammer with a strong right arm, but with greater force and much less effort.

The other piece of 'modern' equipment is a fly press and this is not even powered. Greg demonstrated its usefulness. He took a cold steel bar, placed it under the press, twisted the counterbalanced handle above the screw and the rod bent in a smooth curve; he then moved it along, and did the same again. He could

The walls of the forge are hung with objects left behind by generations
of blacksmiths who have worked here over the years.

have gone like this on until it was bent into a perfect circle. These devices make
life easier, but most of the work is still down to hearth, hammer and anvil. The
only other difference between this forge now and how it was when it was new
is the metal itself: originally the smith would have worked with wrought iron,
but very little of that metal is made today. Nowadays virtually all the work uses
mild steel, which has very similar properties, and it would take an extraordi-
narily keen and expert eye to spot the difference in the finished product.

Watching Greg make something as apparently simple as a poker shows
the huge range of techniques that are involved in turning a metal rod into
an object that is at once attractive and useful. It involves using a variety of
tools and jigs, and these are not brought in from outside – he makes them
himself. The whole process starts with heating the metal in the traditional
hearth. When it was originally built, air would have been blown in to raise
the temperature using bellows; now it has a more convenient air pump.
Some techniques are very straightforward, like making a point by hammering the hot metal on the anvil. To make the body of the poker a more
interesting shape, it is twisted and given a decorative top in the form of
a ram's head. The metal is split and curled to form the two horns, and

Waxing a poker after forging.

the actual head created by shaping and welding. The various stages can be seen in the photographs.

At the opposite end of the scale was another work in progress – an ornate gazebo. The uprights had been roughened to give a more organic look, by shaping under the Blacker hammer. The open roof was created in three parts that were then welded together, using an arc welder. Inevitably, this turned out to be yet another piece of venerable equipment, dating from the 1930s. The welds would later be disguised by metal tendrils that would creep all round the frame. The lucky recipient is going to get a real work of art. It epitomises Greg's philosophy – to combine traditional techniques with modern design. What struck me most about the forge was the contrast in the different types of work carried out and the great versatility of the craftsman. At one end of the spectrum were the sculptures carried out with great delicacy and precision. At the opposite extreme was the stove built to heat the workspace, cobbled together from an old calor gas bottle and an iron door made on the spot. He does exactly what needs to be done for each job, whether it is meeting the exact requirements of a client or making something strictly practical for his own use. This surely is one of the key differences between this sort of work and that produced in more modern factories: there is no standardisation, everything is individually crafted and each customer gets something unique.

CB

Left: Flattening a metal rod using the powered Blacker hammer, a machine that was probably manufactured more than half a century ago.

Different stages in creating a ram's head poker. In the main picture, the hot metal is being split open with a chisel. After that the two parts are spread out to create the ram's horns. The poker is given a decorative chest. The final result is a very convincing ram's head at one end of the poker.

The Foundry

The Ironbridge Gorge area of Shropshire is a World Heritage Site thanks to events that happened here in the early 18th century. It was at Coalbrookdale, close to the town of Ironbridge itself, that Abraham Darby first smelted iron using coke and used the metal to cast objects in sand. He made round-bellied cooking pots, the traditional ware used when cooking was largely done over open fires. Today, right next to the original Darby works, parts for a more modern cooking appliance, the Aga cooker, are being cast.

The Aga is often thought of as quintessentially British, but it was actually invented by a Swedish physicist, Dr Gustav Dalen, managing director of the Swedish Gas Accumulator Company – Svenske Aktiebolaget Gasaccumulator – which gave the initials AGA to his device. It came about through an industrial accident that left Dalen kicking his heels at home, where he realised just how much effort his wife had to make to keep their old oven going with solid fuel. So he set out to design his new kitchen range, in which temperature was controlled via a thermostat and the oven was heavily lagged, and the only escape for heat was through holes in the top, closed by insulated lids until it was time to cook. Manufacture began in Britain at the Coalbrookdale works and has been going on there ever since.

Casting was originally carried out by making a wooden pattern of the part to be cast, then placing it in a moulding box and packing it round with special sand that would hold its shape once the pattern was removed. The resulting space was then filled with molten iron to produce an exact replica of the original. This process is very similar to that already described for the bell foundry. Today, patterns are generally made from aluminium rather than wood, but otherwise little has changed, and in one department where prototypes are being made for testing, the molten metal is still poured by hand. Abraham Darby would have felt quite at home here.

Above: The Aga factory in Coalbrookdale, Shropshire.

Right: Filling the reservoir with molten iron that will then be dropped in controlled amounts into the moulds passing underneath on the conveyor belt.

Most of the raw material for the foundry comes from old cast iron gearboxes that will be melted down in the furnace.

Tapping the furnace: the molten metal is being poured into a ladle that will then be wheeled away to the production line.

The first thing a visitor to the works sees outside the buildings is a pile of scrapped gearboxes from old cars. These will be melted down in the furnace, together with other scrap including, on occasion, parts of old Agas. Limestone is also added to act as a flux to remove impurities, together with special additives, including magnesium and silicon, to provide just the right qualities for high-level casting. The furnace is a voracious monster that requires constant feeding. Throughout the day scrap iron is lifted up the tall tower on a mechanical hoist and emptied into the open top. At the bottom of the tower a constant stream of molten metal pours into a container and every few minutes a forklift truck trundles along with an oversized metal bucket. The container is tapped,

the iron flows out in a flurry of sparks and the bucket is then carried away, spluttering and flaming, to the production line.

When I first visited this factory many years ago, individual casting boxes were laid out on the foundry floor, and the metal was brought to them, to be poured individually. Now the process has been reversed: the moulds are loaded onto a conveyor that brings them underneath the vat filled with the molten iron from the furnace. As each box appears under the vat, the conveyor stops briefly and a carefully controlled amount of molten metal drops into a pipe poking up from the top of the box, known as the running system. Then it moves off, spouting flames. The little train of moulds moves slowly on its way like some odd, candlelight procession. As the moulds cool

For some small items the moulds are still filled by hand.

down, they are broken up and the different parts separated for reuse. The sand goes one way, the casting another. At the next stage, the castings are separated from the running system, which also goes off for reuse: nothing is ever wasted.

At this stage, the castings look not very much better than the scrap piled up outside, but that soon changes. First they are sandblasted, then they are sent to have rough edges ground away and to be given a final polish. The different components are then sent away for assembly at nearby Ketley. At the end of the day, there is one final spectacle to enjoy – the drop. The bottom of the furnace is opened up and all the remaining metal and slag falls out with a spectacular fireworks display.

A traditional Aga cooker.

The
Clockmaker

Ashbourne in Derbyshire has been a centre of clockmaking for centuries, and the Haycock family have been part of it for centuries as well. The story begins when John and Thomas Haycock went to work for the Ashbourne clockmakers Harlow, who had started in the business back in 1740. In 1826 they took over the firm and changed the name to Haycock. In 1865, William Haycock decided to set up in business on his own and by 1897 he was well enough established to move to brand-new works, and William Haycock Ltd have been there ever since, today with Neil Haycock, a sixth-generation Haycock, in charge. Walking into the works today, you could easily think that very little has changed, and in many ways you would not be wrong.

This is a typical 19th-century industrial building, of musty red brick. Climbing the stone steps, worn into scooped-out shapes by generations of workmen's boots, you enter the workshop itself, crammed from end to end with machines, some of which look as if they might have been there when the works were started – and some of them really are almost that old, and one is a good deal more ancient. And it's not just the machines that look historical: the method of working them dates back to an older age. It is not often these days that, other than in a museum, you will find an engineering workshop where machines are run by belts from overhead line shafting. Originally the power source was a gas engine, later replaced by an oil engine and today an electric motor does the job. In the old days, a huge amount of work was done by hand. The workmen were given files, which had to be perfectly maintained: once a file got worn it could still be used on steel, but not on brass. At one workstation, a secret drawer was discovered that could only be opened with a hidden catch: some crafty worker was making sure no one took his file when he wasn't looking. A degree of mechanisation took over some of the tasks, including the manufacture of two key components of any clock, the wheels and pinions.

One of the main types of clock made here is the hook and spike wall clock. It hangs from the hook, and the face is kept vertical by two spikes at the back of the clock that hold it away from the wall. The power is produced by a falling weight turning a drum, and regulated by the pendulum swinging to and fro at a pace that will set the timing of the clock. This

Left: Clockmaker Neil Haycock in his workshop, where many of the machines are still driven by overhead line shafts and belts.

Above: Among the most intricate work that Neil takes on is making skeleton clocks with their elaborate tracery.

Opposite: Neil turning a spindle on one of his lathes.

motion then has to be conveyed to hands moving round the dial through the gear train, a series of wheels and pinions. Good, accurately made and set gear wheels are essential to the accurate working of any clock, and they govern the speed at which the hands move. Obviously, the minute hand has to move exactly 60 times the speed of the hour hand. And both the wheel and the pinion have to be engineered with great accuracy. One can easily imagine the frustration of someone cutting a large wheel with 200 teeth only to make a mistake on the last tooth and the whole thing having to be scrapped. The machines in regular use for preparing these components have both already passed their 100th birthday.

The pinion is a shaft that is turned through gear teeth that carry the motion of the pendulum on to the gear wheel and thus eventually move the hands. It is made of steel, and the first part of the process involves the special pinion-cutting machine. There are two cutters normally in use, the rough cutter and the finishing cutter. The movement is controlled by an 'index', a metal plate that controls the action of the cutters that cut the teeth of the drive according to the number of teeth needed. There are different plates for different pinions. That is by no means the end of the story. The pinion

now has to be hardened, by heating it up to cherry red, then quenched in oil. This process distorts the pinion, so now it has to be tempered by being burned in a special oil, and then it is taken over to a vice, and the pinion laid in a groove. It's now hammered along its side and the hammering process stretches the steel on that side, and the craftsman keeps working at it until the pinion is true again.

The first machine for cutting wheels for clocks was made in the 18th century by John Whitehurst, one of the eminent group of industrialists and scientists that included men such as Josiah Wedgwood and James Watt, who made up the Lunar Society of Birmingham. He built a wheel-cutting machine for his clockmaking business in Derby and when it was finally

discarded, long after Whitehurst himself had died, Neil's great-great-grandfather bought it. Perhaps the most surprising feature is the fact that the actual cutter is driven by nothing more exotic than a loop of string, joining the large wheel on the line shafting to the far smaller wheel on the cutter itself. And here it is, still in working order. The more modern version again uses an index – the mechanical equivalent of a computer program – to cut the teeth by moving the disc round one notch after each cut. The wheels are attached to their pinions on another specialist machine, which rolls over the end of the pinion above the wheel.

Another speciality of the family business in times gone by that has been revived is the skeleton clock. It gets its name because it is a free-standing

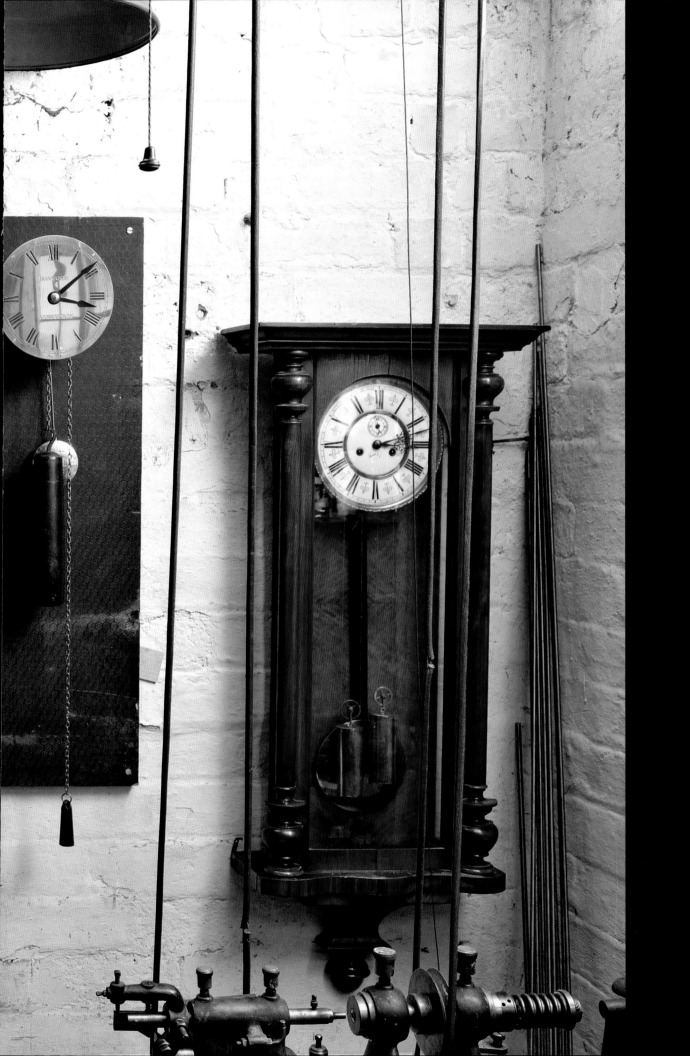

A selection of clocks, including fou[...]
of Haycock's special wall clocks.

Above: The 19th century workshops of William Haycock Ltd in Ashbourne, Derbyshire

Opposite: Neil checking the accuracy of his work on the gear-cutting machine.

clock but one with an open case so that the mechanism is on view. Neil used the original as a pattern to cut the elaborate frames by hand.

This is only a sample of the machines that are regularly in use for both building new clocks and repairing the old. Some even have their own little historical quirks. One lathe, built during the Second World War, still has its instruction booklet, with details of how to blow it to smithereens in the event of an invasion. What all these machines have in common is that they are designed for precision and are a reminder that the clockmakers were the first precision engineers, which is why when something works to perfection we still say it goes like clockwork. There's an interesting juxtaposition here. When Richard Arkwright designed the first machines in the world that would take the manufacture of cotton out of the home and into a water-powered factory in the 18th century, he needed someone to manufacture the parts, so he advertised for clockmakers. More than two centuries later a museum in Germany decided to build replicas of the Arkwright machinery – and the job came here to the Haycock workshop. The special skills of the clockmaker are still appreciated. One can acquire electric and electronic clocks that keep time superbly, but for many people they will never have the appeal of the ticking clock with its intricate network of moving parts. As long as superb craftsmanship is appreciated, there will be a role for the clockmaker. *CB*

The Miner

Coal mining may not seem to have very much to do with working metal, but without an appropriate fuel it is not even possible to extract the metal from its ore in the first place. For centuries, metal working in forge and foundry has relied on coal to provide the necessary heat, either in the form in which it was dug from the earth or transformed into coke. Mining was one of the country's most important and prosperous industries, but that changed in the years of the Thatcher government, with the massive programme of pit closures. One group of miners, however, enjoys independence that has been enshrined in law since the 13th century – the Free Miners of the Forest of Dean. The rights were granted during the reign of Edward I in his war with the Scots. The King's forces were besieging the fortress town of Berwick-upon-Tweed with little success until miners from the Forest tunnelled their way under the walls. It was decreed that any man who had been born in the Hundred of St Briavels and had worked underground for a year and a day could register as a Free Miner with rights to mine in the Forest. The rule has never been revoked and is still exercised to this day.

Robin Morgan is a Free Miner who qualified easily for the necessary period of work underground by bunking off school to help his brothers. Now at an age when most men have retired, he still works his own mine, Hopewell Colliery, as he has for the past two decades. The deep pits that once employed large numbers of men have long since closed and the remaining mines are, like Robin's, entered via long, sloping tunnels rather than down vertical shafts. Part of the mine is open to visitors and part is still very much a working colliery, producing coal that is sold locally.

Tunnelling through solid rock is demanding work, so approach tunnels are no larger than absolutely necessary, which means that going down the mine involves walking with a Groucho Marx-like crouch to avoid rattling your helmet on the roof. And as you descend, the light dims and you are left with just the glow from the helmet lamp. The seam of coal is followed and the covering rock blasted away with gelignite. The seam is a mere three feet thick, with just enough space to set an automatic cutter in place. But that only loosens the coal. Robin has to crawl in and lie on his side to shovel the coal into the waiting tubs, known as 'drams'. It is dirty, uncomfortable

Robin Morgan in his Forest of Dean mine; the coal seam can be seen sloping away up to the right by the chute.

Above: Getting coal from the face to the surface is made easier by using cable-hauled trucks.

Opposite: The winding gear for the cable, powered by an old Morris Marina car engine.

work, and the closest thing to a pithead bath is a wash in the clear stream that flows at the bottom of the mine.

Once a dram is loaded and got into position, it can be hauled to the surface by cable. The winding drums were once powered by powerful steam engines; at Hopewell, however, power comes from a Morris Marina engine that last saw the inside of a car bonnet over 30 years ago. The financial rewards for all this work are negligible, so why does Robin keep going? The answer is pride in a long tradition that is in danger of dying out and eventually being forgotten. It is a tradition of hard and dangerous work that few of us would want to undertake, and in a nearby part of the Forest you will find a monument to the men who died when Union Pit flooded. They and their work deserve to be remembered.

The Printed Word

The Paper Mill

The approach is not quite what you might expect for an industrial site: turning off a main road, you take a very minor road to the village of Roadwater, then turn off onto a single-track road that winds its way beside a little river, and when that peters out into a muddy track, you have arrived. Pitt Mill. With its attached mill house, this is a sturdy building sitting snugly between wooded hillsides, alongside the river that for centuries provided all the power it needed. This is the home of the Two Rivers Paper Company. It was originally built as a grain mill, and has been here for at least 400 years. Walking inside, it's easy to sense that all those years have passed by. Like so many old buildings it has a very special atmosphere, and shows the slow passage of time: floors are no longer quite even and beams are lower than they would be in any modern building – it is all too easy to bang your head in here if you're not careful. But most importantly it looks like a working site, not like a museum with everything neatly tidied away. And there is also a very good clue as to what this mill now makes: every spare piece of wall has a water-coloured painting or print on it. The owner and manager Jim Patterson is a keen watercolourist and a fourth-generation paper maker; here he has combined his passions to produce hand-made paper, specifically designed to meet the needs of artists.

Paper was first made in China over 2,000 years ago, and it is a tribute to the resilience of hand-made paper that examples have survived right down to the present day. The manufacturing principles are the same today as they were then. The one difference is the introduction of power sources to parts of the process. The use of water mills in paper making started over a thousand years ago, and Pitt Mill still has its waterwheel, though it was temporarily out of commission. It was hoped to have it restored and working some of the machinery again quite soon.

Above: Pitt Mill, now home to the Two Rivers Paper Company.

Opposite: Lifting the mould out of the tank containing the mixture of cotton fibre and paper, leaving a sheet of paper formed on the wire mesh.

Mixing bleached cotton with water to create the slurry
from which the paper will be formed.

Paper making begins with the raw material, a natural product containing cellulose. In the past, this mainly came from rags, collected street by street by the rag-and-bone man. In later years, as more and more synthetics came in, it became increasingly difficult to find rags made of pure materials, such as cotton and linen, so today the mill mainly relies on imported bleached cotton that comes in the form of thin boards known as lintels. Just like the rags, however, these have to be broken down. The larger of two machines is an 1841 Hollander rag breaker, the machine that was until recently powered by the large overshot waterwheel. There is also a smaller rag breaker, worked by electricity. Rags are still sometimes used. One of the paintings in the mill shows birds against a blue background – and the blue is not added. It is the paper itself that has been coloured by adding chopped-up blue cotton jeans to the mix.

The beaten material is mixed with water to create the basic slurry from which the paper will be made. This stage is crucial, because the paper has to be just the right thickness and density. It is measured in grams per square

Finished sheets of paper being hung up to dry.

metre (g/m²). To the non-expert these figures don't mean very much, but to put them into perspective, the paper we all buy for our computer printers is around 80-90g/m²; the paper made here varies from 300 to 630g/m². This is seriously thick, robust paper. To get the right consistency depends on three factors. The first is the setting of the rag breaker. Inside the case is a ribbed roller that does the work, and the space between that and the base plate can be adjusted to produce different-sized fragments. The mix will also depend on the amount of time the material spends in the breaker, and

finally on the ratio of pulped matter to water. Other material is also added, including an acid-free size and chalk to make the mixture alkaline. The final mix takes place in the stuff tank, which is just what the name suggests: a tank with stuff in it. Then once all is ready, the mixture is run into an open-topped tank, and now the paper can be made.

The paper is quite literally made by hand using a mould. This consists of an oblong frame, the deckle, holding a wire mesh of phosphor bronze, a material that does not corrode in water. Most of the moulds used here

Left: The entrance to the mill with the owner's house to the side.

Opposite: Dropping a sheet of paper from the mould onto felt: a pile of alternating felts and paper will go to the press to remove the last of the water.

are specially made for the mill, and the mesh is actually woven on a 19th-century loom. The paper maker, Neil Hopkins, dips the mould into the mixture, then raises it horizontally, and with a few deft movements allows the thick liquid to spread evenly over the mould, where it meshes together to form a sheet. This will not have the clean edges of cut, machine-made paper, and many artists prefer to keep it this way, the deckle edges adding the distinctive mark of hand-made paper.

At the next stage, they depart from tradition, but as Jim pointed out, this is not a museum dedicated to preserving traditional ways, but a working mill that needs to show a profit. They use the hand-making process because they cannot get such superb results any other way, but if part of the process can be speeded up using new technology then that is what they'll do. So, the first step on the paper's journey is to place the mould onto a vacuum table that sucks out some of the water. This is a quick process, and the mould is then inverted over a felt. Traditionally, felts were woollen blanket pieces, but here the fabric is backed with plastic to make it firmer and less likely to move, causing the paper to wrinkle up. So a stack of alternating paper sheets and felts is built up, and when the stack is full it is slid under a hydraulic press. This squeezes out about half of the remaining moisture.

The watercolour paper is plain, but special papers can also be made. During our visit, Neil Hopkins was at work on an order of 2,500 sheets for the Museum Plantin in Antwerp. They wanted their own watermark in the paper. Watermarks are produced by stitching the device into the centre of the mesh. When it is dipped into the tank, paper accumulates over the watermark, but in the drying process this evens out, leaving a mark that can only be seen when the paper is held up to the light.

The paper is now firm enough to be handled and can be peeled off the felts. For the next part of the drying process, the paper is taken to the top floor of the mill and a different process begins. This time the stack consists of alternating sheets of paper and corrugated board, with a weight on top. Warm air is blown through. There is one other addition to the paper still to be made. At this stage, the size has made the paper waxy and this would hold back the paint, so it is dipped into animal gelatine. The sheets have to be quickly separated and hung up individually from racks suspended from the ceiling. Only then, when they are completely dry, is the process complete, some three days after it started.

In this mechanised and computerised age, this may seem like an unwieldy and ridiculously old-fashioned way to make paper. It is not necessarily the best paper that can be made – as Jim says, paper made for toilet rolls is the best for what is asked of it. This is quite simply the best you can get for painting with water colours. Again quoting Jim – it is forgiving. It allows the artist to manipulate the paint in different ways; it won't scuff up when treated harshly. It is unquestionably expensive, not because of the price of the materials, but purely because of the time it takes. Amateurs often ask if it is worth it for them to invest in it, to which Jim would reply – yes, simply because it will make your work easier and ultimately better. Jim regularly goes to art shows and he reckons to be able to recognise work that has used his paper: the colours have a brilliance and clarity that is unique.

This is the last purely commercial mill in Britain still making paper by hand, and it survives for two closely related reasons: the passion of its owner for making the very best quality paper, and the demand from serious artists for his unique product.

The Printer

Printing has been transformed in the electronic age. We can all print a clean, neat page of type with a click of the mouse. So why would anyone want to go back to an older technology: letterpress printing? The answer is not simple, but I can start to answer it with a quotation, the title of a novel by Anthony Powell: *Books Do Furnish a Room*, the 10th in the sequence of 12 novels that make up his masterpiece, *A Dance to the Music of Time*. Certainly books furnish almost every room in my house, but just as furniture can be crafted to become a thing of beauty or may simply be a piece of mass-produced ugliness, so too books can be cheap and cheerful or objects to cherish. Of course, the first essential for any book is that the contents are worthwhile, but beyond that there is a special pleasure in owning a book that has been produced with loving care. Printers and publishers Whittington Press, founded in 1971 and still run by John Randle, do just that, and visiting them helps towards an understanding of why the older technology is not just surviving, but becoming increasingly popular.

The press takes its name from the Gloucestershire village of Whittington and actually stands in the grounds of the Elizabethan manor house, Whittington Court. The press building started life as a cottage, became a sawmill, then for a time housed the generator to provide electricity for the great house. It has been extended over the years. A stone-built single-storey building, it hides away modestly behind a barrier of trees. Even before you step inside there is a hint of what goes on here. Over the years stone carvers have visited the press and have been invited to carve lettering into the wall, a reminder of what our script owes to the inscriptions carved on Roman monuments. This rather peaceful, ordered exterior does not, however, prepare anyone for what they will find inside – a series of rooms packed with machinery, pictures everywhere, proofs of illustrations and script scattered around and a general sense of satisfyingly organised chaos.

The principles of letterpress printing haven't changed in their essentials since the system was invented by Johann Gutenberg in the 15th century and John reckons that if Gutenberg walked in today he would have no real problems in getting down to work. Gutenberg's system of movable type consisted of casting the individual characters in metal, which could then be set in order in a fixed frame and inked. The paper would then be pressed

Patrick Randle, son of the founder of Whittington Press, on one of the larger presses.

against the inked frame to create a page of script.

The first stage in the process is composition. Traditionally this was done by hand, and at Whittington some work is still done this way. This is mostly for producing posters, which give John an opportunity to use a wide range of different type sizes – although most type is metal, for the larger letters, generally above 72pt (more than 25mm), wood is used. The pieces of type are themselves rather beautiful objects. The compositor has two cases of type, the upper for capital letters, the lower for the rest – hence upper and lower case. The individual letters, punctuation marks and so on are set in a 'stick', a character at a time, with spacing supplied by lead slivers. This is a skilled job. For a start, the compositor has to learn to set things backwards, because when the impression is made on the paper it will be reversed. Because most books are set with justified text, aligned at both edges, great care has to be taken with getting a good spacing that is agreeable to the eye, avoiding

awkward word and line breaks. When each stick is complete it is added to a frame and once the frame is complete it is locked in place ready for printing.

The first press that was used is a wonderful creation, a Columbian, built in America by Clymer and Dixon in 1848. The massive cast-iron frame is a riot of decoration, embossed with a cornucopia and the staff of Mercury, and topped by a gilded bald-headed eagle. The latter is more than a patriotic emblem: it acts as a counterweight, for the whole system is based on a lever. This is a flatbed press, in which the press descends vertically to press the paper to the typeface. What is astonishing is the perfect balance. The operator pulls a handle and the whole thing moves, slowing towards the end to give maximum control. This was the press on which John Randle printed his very first book. It is no longer in use, but who could possibly get rid of such an amazing piece of machinery?

There is one disadvantage of hand setting, apart from the rather slow

Above: The keyboard produces punched type that provides the instructions for turning molten lead into type on the casting machine.

Right: Type ready for printing as a galley proof.

Opposite: The compositor is setting up type on the keyboard of a monotype machine.

laboriousness of the process: with time, the type becomes worn and loses its crispness. It was inevitable that some day hand setting of type would be replaced by some sort of machine, and the monotype setter made its first appearance in the 1880s, designed in America by Tolbert Lanston and later improved by John Sellars Bancroft. The system also solved the problem of worn type, since each piece of type was individually cast and used just once. The compositor now works at a keyboard which has been described as the familiar QWERTY keyboard on steroids, with different keys for upper- and lower-case roman and upper- and lower-case italic as well as other necessities such as numerals and punctuation marks. I am writing on a typical computer keyboard; the monotype board is like five of these stuck together. When a key is pressed it produces a hole in a paper role – very similar to the way in which pressing a piano key provided the old-fashioned piano roll.

The roll provides the instructions for casting the type. A matrix case is a metal plate consisting of a grid of 15 by 15 characters. This is placed in the caster, which is fed by molten lead. The punched tape feeds the correct character from the matrix over the mould, the lead is poured and a piece of type is formed. This ingenious machine also has a mechanism for mak-

ing the fine adjustments needed for justifying the print. It is fascinating to watch in operation as a line of glistening type appears, a character at a time, in perfect order. When the Oxford University Press abandoned letterpress printing, John acquired their stock of matrices, which are now housed in row upon row of boxes, giving him not only a huge choice of typefaces, but also, should the need ever arise, the ability to print books in anything from Ancient Greek to Gaelic.

There are smaller proof presses at the works, which use rollers instead of the older flatbed press. John Randle's son Patrick has joined him in the business; he was working on a job that combined old and new technologies. He was adding letterpress printing to coloured illustrations and was coping with the technical problem of getting his inked surface to adhere to the already formed coloured illustrations. The ink was rolled over the type, the roller moved across and he was experimenting with how much pressure

Left: For short runs a small hand-operated press can be used.

Opposite: John Randle checking on the quality of one of the illustrations before starting the main print run.

was needed to get just the right result. Printing is not just about pushing a button and stepping back.

For book printing the press uses a far grander machine, a Heidelberg press. This is the big brother to the proofing presses, still using a roller but one that weighs in at about a ton. This great mass ensures stability and consistency, yet it is remarkably sensitive – it can be adjusted to the width of a sheet of fine tissue paper. Printing eight pages on each side of a sheet of paper, it is fast and efficient. It is a modern machine – well, modern is a relative term, as it has already passed its fiftieth birthday.

The end result is the printed page and it is here that you can see why letterpress printing survives. The ideal contact between paper and press is the 'kiss impression', the lightest of touches but powerful enough to transfer the ink and make a slight impression. As John Randle says, modern printing is essentially 2D – but this is 3D, and it makes a real difference to the appearance of the printed page, even if it is only just about possible to feel the indentations with one's fingertips. There is also the personal factor. I was reading a book a couple of days ago, set as most are using a computer program, and I came across a page that ended with a hyphenated word – so you had to turn the page to get the rest of it. This is a small point perhaps, but it was irritating, and no letterpress compositor would ever allow such a thing to happen: the spacing would be adjusted to get the whole word on one page or move it all to the next.

CB

The Illustrator

Many of the Whittington Press books are illustrated, most often by Miriam Macgregor, who has been working with the press for many years. Her speciality is the woodcut, a medium that, to be successful, has to combine great craftsmanship with artistic sensibility. It is clear from the end product that Miriam Macgregor has both.

I visited her at her cottage, which is also her studio, half an hour's drive from the press. Unlike some other artists, the specialist in woodcuts requires very little space in which to work. If it wasn't for the small press in the corner and the big magnifying glass on a stand at one end of the desk under the studio window, it could easily be any small office. The apparatus is simple, but not quite what you would expect. As many of us discover, standing up and bending over gets wearing as the years creep up. Traditionally, the block of wood that is being worked on would be placed on a sandbag. The actual cutting uses a combination of moving the tool with one hand while rotating the block with the other. Miriam has an improvised system: a sloping desk, on which she has fixed a small turntable, originally used by a potter for finishing his ware. She fastens her block to the turntable and can sit comfortably to work.

She studied art at Hastings, which was where she first saw woodcuts – and was not impressed. As a student she wanted to work on a huge scale, not producing tiny images. After college she worked in advertising – which she hated – then moved into publishing and eventually came to the Whittington Press, initially as a compositor, but it was there she found her vocation as an illustrator. She has never had any great ambition to be a gallery artist: her métier is, and remains, as an illustrator. She has a wonderful eye for the odd and quirky – I particularly loved a book she illustrated devoted to allotments, which brought individuals to life as well as the strange array of sheds they create for themselves. To me, that is the beauty of woodcuts: they lend themselves to the celebration of individuality. But I remain amazed by the skill required in producing them. It involves what I would regard as thinking backwards. If you do a sketch, you draw a line on paper; but in a woodcut, you have to do the reverse, cut around that line so that it stands proud from the block. The tools used are delicate, thin-bladed

Miriam Macgregor at work on a woodcut – she uses the turntable to create smooth curves.

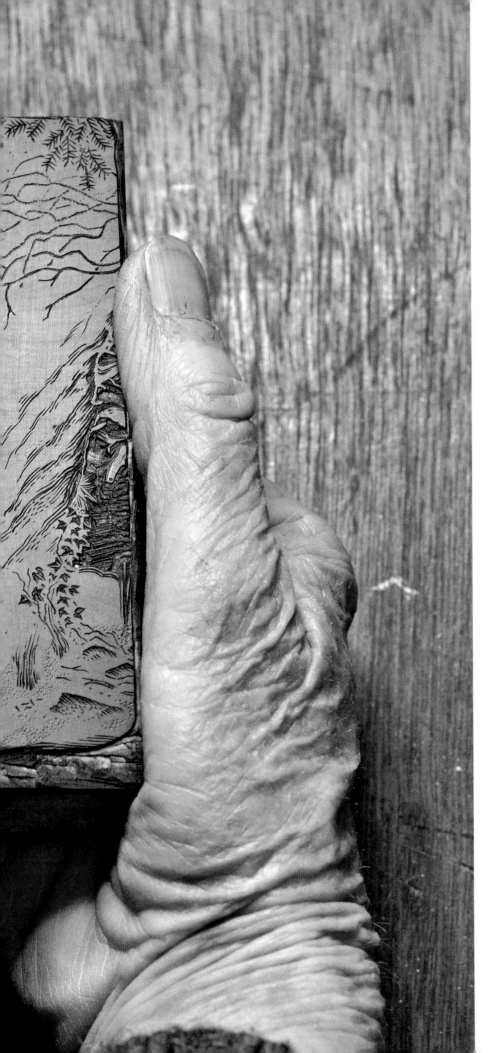

Above: The printed version as it will appear in the finished book.

Opposite: The completed engraving of Whittington Church, carved in reverse.

knives, one of which has the rather bizarre name of spit sticker. She was currently working on a book based on the local Whittington Church, and she had a partially completed block. The detail on it was just incredibly fine – and there is no room for error. It was a pleasant coincidence to find, when we visited the bookbinders sometime later, that this was the actual book they were working on.

Miriam has recently adopted a new technique, which is certainly no simpler than woodcutting, known as pochoir. This involves cutting stencils in order to produce a coloured image. One stencil lays down one colour, then the next stencil covers a different area to put down a different colour and so on. One image required 14 different stencils, and it only needs one of those to be misaligned to ruin the whole thing. But the results are worth it. And that surely is the point of reviving and using these techniques: the images produced are unique, totally unlike those produced in any other medium.

Producing the printed words and the illustrations to accompany them is only a part of the process involved in turning ideas into books. The results have to be bound together. *CB*

The
Bookbinder

The Fine Book Bindery does not present an imposing façade to the world – it is a typically nondescript modern industrial building in a suburban street in Finedon in Northamptonshire. Inside, however, is very different: this is the home of true craftsmanship and it must be one of the most cheerful workplaces I have ever visited. This is almost certainly due to two factors: these are people producing objects of great beauty, and they are a team that has been together for a very long time. But the story of that team nearly ended a few years ago.

One of the founding members, Maurice Edwards, began a six-year apprenticeship as a bookbinder in Dagenham in 1963 and has worked in the industry ever since. In 1987 he and a partner set up their own company, the Fine Bindery, in Wellingborough. The aim was to provide a service that would use the highest standards of craftsmanship to produce luxuriously bound books. By 2007, however, they were in severe financial difficulties. Their plight came to the attention of Patrick Roe. He had started printing as an enthusiastic teenager and by now had his own company, the Logan Press. Instead of buying the old company, he set up a new one, the Fine Book Bindery, and invited Maurice and his whole team to join him. They did and here they are still, including Maurice himself, practising their craft.

Work begins when the printed sheets arrive from the printers. A typical sheet will have 16 pages of print, 8 on one side and 8 on the other. All the sheets are then folded, each folded sheet being known as a signature. These now have to be stitched together. This is normally done on a machine, very similar to the familiar domestic sewing machine, except that it has a row of needles and bobbins. Each movement of the foot treadle produces a complete row of stitches. In a few cases, the stitching is actually done by hand. At this stage, the sheets are still folded, so the individual pages have to be cut open. In the more distant past, books were sold with the pages uncut. Years ago, while researching in the Bodleian Library in Oxford, I ordered up a book which still had its pages uncut, which meant that, rather sadly, no one had looked at it in the two and a half centuries it had sat on their shelves. Here the pages are sliced open on a guillotine: it is obviously easier to do the whole set in one

Stitching the pages of the book on Whittington Church illustrated by Miriam Macgregor.

Above: The sheets from the printer come with more than one page per sheet – on this side four pages can be seen.

Right: After the pages have been stitched and glued, the edges are rounded off.

slice rather than do it a sheet at a time before stitching.

As well as being stitched, the pages are glued. In order for the sewn pages to fit snugly into the spine, one edge is rounded off. First of all it is beaten gently into shape with a special hammer with a domed head instead of the usual flat head. Then the sheets go to the backing machine. The operator drops the sheets down between the jaws of a clamp and adjusts their position from below by hand. When they are in the correct position, he uses a foot treadle to close the clamp and hold them firmly in position. He then pulls on a handle to work a roller backwards and forwards to smooth the edge.

In another part of the works, the outer case is being prepared. The case being worked on during our visit was, very appropriately, the Whittington Press publication about Whittington Church, featuring woodcuts by Miriam Macgregor. This had been printed on one of the smaller presses, with just 8 pages to the sheet. The case design simulated an ornate hinge from the door of a church. This would be created on the case using two different-coloured goatskin pieces. The design was sent out to a specialist firm, who created a cutter of exactly the size and shape of the hinge outline. The lighter leather was then laid on the board that would form the casing and the cutter used to remove a section of leather corresponding

The cover motif, representing an ornate hinge on a church door, is created from two different shades of leather. A shaped cutter is used so that one piece of coloured leather can be fitted accurately into the background leather. The final result is this handsome cover and when the book is opened it reveals Miriam Macgregor's woodcut of the church.

to the hinge shape. Cutting the darker leather was slightly more complicated. Leather is an expensive commodity and you want to get as many pieces of the awkward shape out of the skin as possible: it is rather like fiddling with pieces of a jigsaw to make them fit. Once again, the shape is cut and the dark leather now has to be fed slowly into the space left in the lighter layer and carefully glued. Once in place and firmly stuck down, the assembly is placed in a heated press, which gives a smooth, glossy finish. It is now time for the different parts to be united.

The first step is to paste mull, a form of sized cotton cheesecloth, along the spine, which is then allowed to dry. The sewn pages are aligned correctly with the casing, the end papers added and the board covers folded into place and glued. The completed volume now has to be pressed. The size of the book will determine which of a number of different presses is used and the length of time it stays compressed, which, in the case of large volumes, can be as long as 24 hours.

Many of these books will be given a handsome slipcase. Each case is made by hand: the cardboard pieces are cut and covered with a velvety material to form a smooth lining and then glued together. The end product is more than just another book: it is a work of art in its own right.

CB

201

What We Wear

The
Woollen Mill

For centuries almost all the clothing worn in Britain was made from wool. Workers in cottages carried out all the preliminary stages: women and children carding and spinning, men weaving. The cloth from the loom was liable to be greasy and, if not treated, would shrink when it got wet. It was treated with fuller's earth to clean it, and stamped on repeatedly in water to shrink it – the origin of the common surname Walker. (The word 'fuller' is derived from 'fulling' – cleaning – wool, the task of those textile workers known as fullers.) These last processes were mechanised in the medieval period in water-powered fulling mills. The wheel turned immense hammers, fulling stocks, that pounded the wool in the water mixed with the cleansing agent. Where there were sheep and water for power, there were clothiers and fulling mills. Wales had ample supplies of both.

A fulling mill, or pandy as it was known in Wales, was built in 1829 on the busy river Crafnant that flows down the hillside to the village of Trefriw in Snowdonia, and was just one of several different kinds of mill powered by the same water. In 1859 it was bought by Thomas Williams and the business has remained in the family ever since. The 18th and early 19th centuries saw great changes in the whole textile industry: first, spinning and carding were mechanised, and shortly after that the power looms were introduced. Work began to move from the home to the factory, and Trefriw Woollen Mills has moved with the times. Today the enterprise is run by brother and sister Morgan and Elaine Williams, and in an age when textile mills – especially woollen mills – were closing all over Britain, something had to be done to stay in business. The answer was to build a new mill on the valley floor, but with a large shop to sell what was produced. The result is that they are still manufacturing, running through the whole range of processes from spinning to weaving. Ironically, the only operation not carried out here is the one the original pandy was built for: if cloth needs finishing it is sent to Scotland. I went round the mill with Morgan Williams, and it was a journey into the textile past. Many of the machines, although scarcely modern, are new in terms of the long history of textile manufacturing, but if a mill owner from the 19th century had come back here, there was little he'd have failed to understand.

Morgan Williams weighing wool at the Trefriw Woollen Mills.

The wool needs to be carded by this machine that disentangles and aligns the fibres.

After carding the wool can be spun into yarn on the spinning mules – the moving carriage draws out the fibres that are then twisted together.

The obvious starting point is the power source. This is still essentially a water-powered mill, but where in the predecessor the water had turned a wheel to power the machinery directly, here it turns a turbine attached to a generator to provide electricity. Everything came to a standstill during a recent harsh winter, when the water that came down 340 metres from lakes high in the hills froze and burst the pipe. It has been repaired, but in the process there has been a loss of power. Fortunately, there is still enough to keep things running, for without this source of energy the whole works would struggle to survive.

Now we started going through all the different processes, beginning in the blending shed, where the wool is delivered. The wool has been packed in bales, squashed up, and now it is laid down, layer by thin layer, and oiled. You can see how deeply the wool is stacked by the oil stains that rise up the wall. Next it needs to be loosened in a machine whose name says it all – the shaker, basically a drum with teeth. It also has to be thoroughly mixed together with a tenterhook machine, a name that meant something quite different to me. Tenterhooks were originally the hooks on a tenter frame, on which cloth was stretched and dried. But I wasn't about to argue with a man who had been in the business all his life. This one passes the wool through toothed rollers to mix the lumps together. From here it is blown through a duct over to bins in the main mill building for the next process.

The mixed wool is still tangled, and in order to be turned into thread the fibres have to be aligned. Originally, this was done by hand, drawing the wool between a pair of cards, objects looking rather like table tennis bats studded with wire. The process is still known as carding, but now instead of the hand cards, the wool is passed between studded rollers. It is, like so much in this industry, an absolutely fascinating process to watch. The wool can be seen passing through from one set of rollers to the next, until it emerges as a delicate sheet of fibres. There's no date on the machine, but Morgan thinks it was built in the 1920s; yet the basic design goes right back to the 18th century and the first carding engine designed by Sir Richard Arkwright.

The wool fibres are all straightened out and aligned, but there is no strength in them. They now need to be drawn out and twisted together to make thread, and this is done on a pair of spinning mules. These are my favourite industrial machines and I never tire of seeing them at work – though that is probably not the case for their operatives. The wool is fed through rollers at the back of the engine and then passes to 360 bobbins set on spindles on a moving carriage. At the start of the operation, the rollers, moving at different speeds, pull out the threads. The carriage moves away, pulling the wool out still further as it goes. Then the carriage stops, the spindles whirl round and the threads are twisted together. A bar drops down over the row of threads, releasing the tension, and the carriage returns,

Left: Dyed yarn has been wound onto 'cheeses' ready for weaving.

Above: Carding was originally carried out using hand cards studded with wire; now machines have taken over the task.

Left: Warping: individual threads have to be arranged in the correct order to create the required pattern in the finished cloth.

Top right: The bobbins of yarn are arranged on a frame ready for the warping process.

Bottom right: From the warping frame the yarn is wound onto a roller that is then fitted to the back of the loom.

winding the twisted thread onto the bobbins. The operative walks backwards and forwards, retying broken threads, and once the bobbins are full, the whole machine has to stop; the 360 full bobbins are removed, and new ones put in their place and threaded up. As a former operative in a Gloucestershire mill once told me, a spinner didn't need to go to the gym: she walked seven miles a day, backwards and forwards, following the action of the mule. Once again, this is a machine that has its origins in the days of the Industrial Revolution. But these ones are quite modern by Trefriw standards – only 60 or so years old.

From the mule, the wool goes to the doubler, a machine as simple as the mule is complex: it takes two sets of threads and winds them together, but

A brilliant colourscape of dyed wool.

twisting in the opposite direction to the twist from the mule. The result is two-ply wool. At this stage, the wool is ready for dyeing, but because it is tightly wound onto cones, it would be difficult for the dye to penetrate evenly. So now it is wound off the cones to make loose hanks. At the dye house, the wool is washed and then heated up with the dye in a huge vat, and then dried. In the old days, water was heated by means of a coal-fired furnace. The coal would be delivered outside, then had to be shovelled down a shute to the dye-house floor, from where it had to be wheeled to the furnace. That was when the real hard work started, keeping the beast fed with fuel – hardly surprising, then, that this is one area where modernity has crept in. Today, all you have to do is press a button to start the modern gas boiler.

Everything is now ready for the final stage, weaving. Before any actual weaving can begin, the loom has to be prepared by adding the warp threads. These are arranged on a roller at the back of the loom and, greatly simplifying the process, the individual threads are passed through eyes in wires, heddles. These allow threads to be raised and lowered, leaving a gap in between through which the shuttle, containing the weft, can be passed. In case you ever get confused over which is which, here's an old weaver's joke – the warp goes up and down and the weft goes from weft to wight. If a plain cloth is being woven, this is a simple matter, but it becomes more complex when a pattern's being created. For a simple stripe, you could

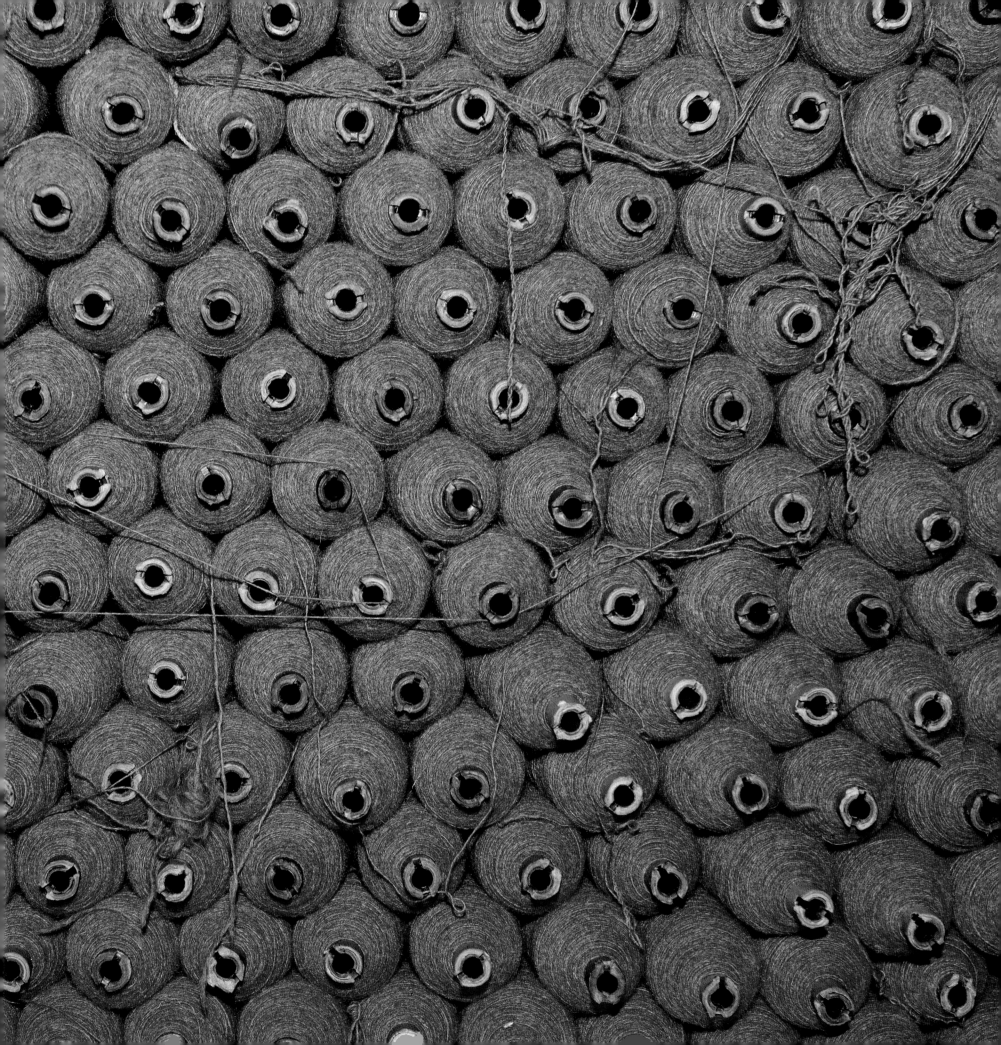

The warp threads are in place on the loom and the weaver is adjusting the weft threads in the shuttle that will move backwards and forwards across the loom to create the weave.

This is a drop-box loom – shuttles with different coloured yard are used to create the pattern in conjunction with the warp.

arrange the warp threads to create bands of colour. For more complex patterns, you also have to change the colours in the weft as well. Once you have your pattern worked out, the threads are wound onto a warping frame that is used to arrange them in the right order on the roller. Originally, it depended on the skill of the weaver to keep changing to different shuttles to create the pattern in the cloth. But here all the work is done on a special type of loom known as a Dobcross. This is an automated system. There are four drop boxes to either side, containing the shuttles. A chain system allows different shuttles to be hurled across in the right order. The cloth grows as you watch, and on this occasion the loom was developing a traditional Welsh pattern for a bedspread. Materials such as this don't require finishing, so go straight to the shop for sale.

Once woollen mills were spread throughout Wales, seldom in the vast units that were found in areas such as Yorkshire, but providing employment for communities throughout the country and especially in rural areas. That Trefriw Woollen Mills has survived is a tribute to the perseverance of many generations of the Williams family: long may it continue. There was a time when woollen mills such as this were to be found in their hundreds, not just in Wales but across Britain, and one centre was Stroud in Gloucestershire, famous for its West of England cloth. Before mechanisation, the cloth would have been made on handlooms, and one might have expected that these would long since have been made obsolete, but Stroud can not only still boast one of the few working mills in the region but also a very successful handloom weaver.

CB

Opposite: The finished cloth being inspected for any possible flaws.

The Tannery

The turning of animal hides into leather by tanning is a craft that goes back to at least Mesolithic times and, as Barry Knight of Thomas Ware & Sons in Bristol said, 'If a tanner from a thousand years ago came back today he'd recognise most of what was going on.' This company may not have been going for a thousand years, but it has been on this site since 1840 and in all those years very little has changed. This is still one of only three traditional vegetable tanneries left in Britain. Seen from the outside, there is very little hint of what is going on inside these really rather nondescript buildings. Inside, however, the atmosphere is strange and unique.

The process begins with the arrival of the carefully selected hides, from either Hereford or Charolais beef cattle. They are stored and packed in salt to preserve them until they are needed. Cows, as anyone walking in the countryside can testify, are not notably hygienic creatures, so the first stage is to clean the hides. This takes place in a series of pits with worn stone edges. The hides are put on a frame that can be raised and lowered into water, and they are left to soak for 24 hours. Then they are moved to a pit with a weak sodium sulphide solution to loosen the hairs, and after that to a series of lime baths to open up the fibrous matter in the skins to allow the tanning solution to penetrate deep into the hide. They stay there for at least six days, while the frames bob slowly up and down to keep the hides moving.

At the end of the soaking, the hides are dragged out by hand. This is very much a two-man operation since by this time the saturated hides weigh at least 75kg each. They work in unison, pulling out a hide, folding it neatly and then returning for the next in a long process. The hides are now fed through two machines that look like monstrous mangles, except that the rollers are fitted with helical blades. The first removes the hairs, which are sold for fertiliser, and the second, the fleshing machine, takes off the fat that goes to make tallow. After that each hide is inspected under a lamp, then quickly marked with reference points and cut by hand. It seems to take no more than a few seconds to make the cuts, and the trimmings are sent off one way and the hide another. This is, in fact, no longer a hide but a pelt, and how it will be used depends on which part of the animal it came from: shoulder, belly or butt. Each pelt is graded and will find its own end

Tanned pelts suspended over the tanning pits at
Thomas Ware & Sons in Bristol.

Above: The hides – now known as pelts – are trimmed before being sent for tanning.

Opposite: After the hair has been removed the hides are soaked in a sodium sulphide solution.

use – some, for example, might go for horse harnesses, another batch for heels for shoes. At this stage they have a high alkaline content, which is neutralised by soaking in dilute acid. Only now are the pelts ready for the long, slow process of tanning.

The first set of pits made an impressive sight, but they are nothing compared with the tanning pits, row upon row, almost 300 in all. The tanning liquid itself is an infusion of tree bark, made just as you would make a pot of tea, if on a vaster scale. Different barks are used for different levels, from the exotic quebracho from South America to oak from a local woodland – but all from sustainable sources. All the solutions are controlled for

composition and temperature depending on the end use. The whole of the tan yard is built with a slightly sloping floor, so that the tanning liquid moves slowly down from the top. The pelts start off at the lowest level, where the tanning liquid is weakest, and are gradually moved up until they are finally removed at the top some six months after they started their journey.

The pelts are now sent to dry in the prosaically named 'sheds'. Direct sunlight would cause damage, so instead of glazed windows the sheds only have shuttered openings. There is room after room of pelts, and one room contained a rather startlingly scarlet set of them. These were destined for a very specialised market: they would finish up as casings for cricket balls. As

Following pages: The start of the process, where the untreated hides are soaked in pits.

these words are being typed, England are playing Pakistan and batsmen are doing their best to knock Thomas Ware's finest leather all round the ground.

Dried leather is oiled and greased in machines that look like either overgrown tumble driers or cement mixers. The finished product can have many different uses: some will be hand-made shoes, some luxury wallets; it can be embossed and even made into floor tiles. The company will produce exactly what the customer wants to the very highest standard – which is why they are still in business after more than a century and a half, and why they still use traditional methods. Nothing else can produce quite that same quality. This has indeed been the theme that has run through all our visits: the different crafts and industries survive simply because they offer character and quality that is unique. Long may they do so.   CB

Top left: The dyed red leather that will be used as the outer casing for cricket balls.

Above left: Patterns marked with shoe sizes that will be used for making leather heels.

Above: Sacks of wood shavings of different kinds, but mainly oak, that will be used in the tanning process.

Opposite: Tanned pelts hung up to dry.

The Sites

Most, but not all, of the sites are open to visitors either on a regular basis or by special arrangement. One or two do not provide contact addresses other than through their website, or prefer not to be listed.

Food for the Table

Claybrooke Water Mill
Frolesworth Lane, Claybrooke Magna, Leicestershire LE17 5DB
www.claybrookewatermill.co.uk

Smart's Farm
Old Ley Court, Birdwood, Gloucestershire GL2 8AR
www.smartsgloucestercheese.com

Fortune's Kippers
22 Henrietta Street, Whitby, North Yorkshire YO22 4DW
www.fortuneskippers.co.uk

Setting the Table

Fletcher Robinson Ltd
34 Lambert Street, Sheffield S3 7AA
www.fletcher-robinson.co.uk

Middleport Pottery
Port Street, Burslem, Stoke-on-Trent ST6 3PE
www.burleigh.co.uk

Two Pints and a Dram

Warminster Maltings
39 Pound Street, Warminster, Wiltshire BA12 8NN
www.warminster-malt.co.uk

Hook Norton Brewery
Brewery Lane, Hook Norton, Oxon OX15 5NY
www.hooky.co.uk

Glenfarclas Distillery
Ballindalloch, Banffshire AB37 9BD
www.glenfarclas.co.uk

Speyside Cooperage
Dufftown Road, Craigellachie, Banffshire AB38 9RS
www.speysidecooperage.co.uk

Brimblecombe's Cider
Farrants Farm, Dunsford, Exeter EX6 7BA

Andrew Gundron, Signature Signs
6 Claylands, St Breward, Bodmin, Cornwall PL30 3PY
www.signaturesignsuk.com

The Church

John Taylor & Co
The Bellfoundry, Freehold Street, Loughborough, Leicestershire LE11 1AR
www.taylorbells.co.uk

Barley Studio
Church Balk, Dunnington, York YO19 5LH
www.barleystudio.co.uk

Henry Willis & Sons Ltd
Rotunda Organ Works, 72 St Anne Street, Liverpool L3 3DY
www.willis-organs.com

Building Materials

Haysom (Purbeck Stone) Ltd
St Aldhem's Quarry, Worth Matravers, Dorset BH19 3LN
www.purbeckstone.co.uk

Salisbury Cathedral
The Close, Salisbury, Wiltshire SP1 2EF
www.salisburycathedral.org.uk/conservation-restoration

Bulmer Brick and Tile
The Brickfields, Bulmer, Sudbury, Suffolk CO10 7EF
www.bulmerbrickandtile.co.uk

English Antique Glass
Bordesley Hall, Alvechurch, Birmingham B48 7QA
www.englishantiqueglass.co.uk

Working Metal

Moreton Forge
27 Cross Street, Moretonhampstead, Devon TQ13 8NL
www.moretonforge.co.uk

Aga-Rayburn Foundry
www.agaliving.com

William Haycock
www.williamhaycock.co.uk

Hopewell Colliery
Cannop Hill, Speech House Road, Coleford, Gloucestershire GL16 7EL
www.hopewellcolliery.com

The Printed Word

Two Rivers Paper Mill
Pitt Mill, Roadwater, Watchet, Somerset TA23 0QS
www.tworiverspaper.co

The Whittington Press
www.whittingtonpress.com

The Fine Book Bindery
21d Orchard Road, Finedon, Northants NN9 5JG
www.finebinding.co.uk

What We Wear

Trefriw Woollen Mills
Main Road, Trefriw, Conwy Valley LL27 0NQ
www.t-w-m.co.uk

Thomas Ware & Sons
Clift House Tannery, Coronation Road, Bristol BS3 1RN
www.thomasware.co.uk

Index